HOW TO CHOOSE A CHURCH

The Church of Christ' Plea for Unity

CARL O. COOPER
1/1/2013

Dedication

This book is dedicated to Lisa Nail. Her tireless efforts to format pages and create covers were a great value to producing this book. She is a dedicated Christian lady who loves God. And she is a valuable member in the kingdom of Christ.

This book is written in a homespun style that editors and proof readers hate. It has been a serious struggle keeping it that way. I hope you hear my voice when you read these words. I hope it is simple to read and easy to understand. It is not written for scholars and preachers and those who have been a part of the church of Christ for many years. It is intended for those who are new to Bible study and new to the church of Christ. I hope that you can consider this book as a hand out to those friends and family members you feel would like to know more about the simple truth of the church of Christ and the New Testament Gospel.

Carl O. Cooper

John 17:20-21 (NKJV)

[20] "I do not pray for these alone, but also for those who will believe in Me through their word; [21] that they all may be one, as You, Father, *are* in Me, and I in You; that they also may be one in Us, that the world may believe that You sent Me.

This is the plea of the churches of Christ

Contents

1. Chapter 1
    How to Choose a Church ....Page 7
2. Chapter 2
    Authority of God .... Page 12
3. Chapter 3
    Do We Have Authority
        To Change God's Plan ....Page 18
4. Chapter 4
    Can Truth Contradict Itself? ....Page 24
5. Chapter
    The Old and New Testament ....Page 33
6. Chapter 6
    The Beginning of the Church ....Page 40
7. Chapter 7
    The Simple Doctrine of
        The Church of Christ ....Page 57
8. Chapter 8
    Born Again ....Page 72
9. Chapter 9
    What about Repentance
        Are All Sins Equal? ....Page 77
10. Chapter 10
    Fundamental principals
        In the church of Christ ....Page 87

Contents *Page 2*

11. Chapter 11
    Instrumental music
    In the church ....Page 93
12. Chapter 12
    We are saved by grace......................Page 102
13. Chapter 13
    Living in a world
    Hostile to Christians ....Page 107
14. Chapter 14
    Why People Seek Religion ....Page 112
15. Chapter 15
    Reasons to Seek God ....Page 119
16. Chapter 16
    Will people be saved
    Who are not members
    Of the church of Christ? ....Page 123
17. Chapter 17
    The Great Falling Away ....Page 129
18. Chapter 18
    Can a saved person be lost? ....Page 135

Chapter 1
How to Choose a Church

How do you know when you have chosen the correct denomination? Many people struggle with this decision. And you can ask your pastors, your preachers, your Sunday school teachers, and anyone you know who claims to teach religion, and they will all tell you that "your feelings are not your guide". And they would be right about that. Your feelings and your emotions are not a proper guide when choosing the proper church.

So if this is the case, and it is, then how do you choose which denomination or which church you align yourself with? Have you ever asked yourself that question or wondered about it? Many people have.

Of course your feelings are not your guide. If they were there would be no wrong answer. Sooner or later every person's conscious becomes acclimated and desensitized to whatever behavior they are associated with. Even sinful behavior will not bother a desensitized conscious after a time.

But someone will say, what about the Holy Spirit? Won't the Holy Spirit guide my feelings to make the right answer? I could give you a long and scholarly answer to the religious doctrine of predestination and irresistible grace but that's too complex for this simple problem of choosing the proper church.

The answer is really simple. How do I choose the proper denomination or church? You use the logical, intellectual, reasoning process that God placed inside your own brain and you find the answer in the Bible. Think about that for a minute. If God had wanted to tell you about a church that He designed and placed on this earth, where would He give this information? Doesn't it make logical sense that God would tell us about this church in the Bible? And that's exactly where the description and the pattern for this church Designed by God is found. It's all there, in the Bible for us to read.

And while we're using our logical reasoning process let's think about that word "denomination". Do you know what it means? Have you even thought about what it means and how it originated? The definition gives a meaningful story about "church division" and "unity". Do you know the plea of Jesus to us just before He died?

John 17:20-21 (NKJV)
[20] *"I do not pray for these alone, but also for those who will believe in Me through their word;*
[21] *that they all may be one, as You, Father, are in Me, and I in You; that they also may be one in Us, that the world may believe that You sent Me.*

When you consider your choice of a church, remember Jesus' dying prayer for us all. The last thing Jesus wanted was division and denominations of His church.

A denomination is a part of something that has been divided. I think you already know that. I think everyone does. The church did not start out as divided. The "original church" was united in their doctrine and was "one" as Jesus and God are united as one. Sure there were false teachers and factions but they were not a part of the true church, they were counterfeit and the Bible describes them as false. The church is under attack by Satan and always has been. In spite of Jesus' prayer for unity false teachers have divided the church from the beginning. There are many hundreds of denominations or divisions established today. So how can we choose the proper church? Simple, go back to the Bible and choose the original.

God has left us a pattern for the design and worship of that "original church". Be cautious here. Many will claim to know what it is and some will even deny that a pattern still exists. But don't be fooled by false teachers about this. The pattern does exist and it is there. **But you will need a teacher to find it.** God has designed that system, too.

Acts 8:30-31 (NKJV)
30 So Philip ran to him, and heard him reading the prophet Isaiah, and said, "Do you understand what you are reading?"
31 And he said, "How can I, unless someone guides me?" And he asked Philip to come up and sit with him.

God has given us His written word and in it He has given us all we need to know to find salvation for our souls, proper everyday living, the pattern for His church and the worship He has designed to be presented to Him. And He has chosen preachers and teachers as a method to help us understand it. Once you have discovered the key to "rightly divide the word of truth" the understanding becomes so much easier that you soon become the teacher yourself.

As I will say many times, the purpose of this book is to help you get started on that search to make sense of the Bible and find the church that God has designed for us all.

You may be new to this concept and you may be asking yourself, why have I not heard about this before? Well the idea is not new by any stretch of the imagination. Jesus thought of it the night he was betrayed and it was in His prayer to God on our behalf. And it has been the plea of the church of Christ every since the first century and still is today. But think about this. Who really wants to teach this concept of the church? Non-Christian religions surely don't. And denominations surely don't. For to teach this concept that eliminates division and a return to the one original church described in the Bible, eliminates all religions and churches but the one. In other words, denominations would cease to exist. Do you know any that would self destruct in order to have one church designed as the original described in the Bible? I think not.

And then there is another side
to this denomination coin.

Once this concept is laid out and described to some churches, they will claim to already be that "original church" described in the Bible. If you are faced with a claim such as this, you may not be able to "rightly divide" the difference if you are new to Bible study and new to the plea of "one body, one church". A good place to start the investigation would be to ask the simple question, "What must I do to be saved"? If they teach any other Gospel other than faith, repentance, confession, and baptism for the remission of sins, then they are not the "original church".

Galatians 1:8 (NKJV)
8 but even if we, or an angel from heaven, preach any other gospel to you than what we have preached to you, let him be accursed.

If you are searching for a church or if you have any reason to suspect that the church you are a part of is just a denomination and not the original church, you need to find a member of the church of Christ and arrange a Bible study. This will not be threatening or disrespectful in any way. We all went through this investigation for ourselves. We know what your questions are because we have asked the same questions ourselves. Don't delay; we will help you investigate just as someone helped us.

The Simple Truth
About The Church of Christ

Chapter 2 *Authority of God*

Does God have authority over the wind?

If you ask this question among those who profess to believe in the one true God, the obvious answer is, yes He does. If you ask the question, does God have authority over the universe, then again the obvious answer is; yes He does. But if you follow this up by asking the question, does God have authority over you; then you might notice some hesitation before the question is answered, but the obvious answer is, once again, yes He does.

So if that is the case, and it is, then what would you expect to do if God asked you to do something? This is such a simple and basic progression of logic that hardly anyone could fail to follow it and understand it. Herein lays the basic foundation and plea of the church of Christ.

With all this in mind, and with the understanding that obedience to the authority of God is the natural order of the universe and everything in it, then we have to decide what we will do with the knowledge of some of the things God has instructed us to do. One such thing and one of a high degree of importance is the prayer of Jesus on the night He was betrayed. As Jesus was making this prayer to God, He was fully aware that He was about to die. In John 17:20-22, Jesus had been praying for

His apostles and He expanded His prayer to include "all those who would believe in me through their word". This includes you and me and all who today believe in Christ. Look at what this verse says;

John 17:20-22 (NKJV)
20 "I do not pray for these alone, but also for those who will believe in Me through their word;
21 that they all may be one, as You, Father, are in Me, and I in You; that they also may be one in Us, that the world may believe that You sent Me.

Teach the Same Doctrine

Could there be any clearer way to tell us that all Christians are to teach the same doctrine? And while the concept of obedience to the will of God is fresh on our minds, what does this scripture do to the pattern of religious division we find in the world today?

People who claim to have a reverence for some form of Christianity in today's world somehow have been led to believe that division in religion is proper and acceptable and even approved by God. And even though there exists hundreds of different denominations of churches who all teach different doctrines and even though many of these doctrines actually contradict each other, people have been taught and conditioned to believe that this is somehow approved by God. And in spite of this scripture which teaches clearly that God's instruction to us is for all to teach the same doctrine and to be one, as God and Christ are one;

People still teach and believe that one church's doctrines are as good as another and in some unknown way, all are true and approved by God. With these 2 verses of scripture in plain, full view, what an amazing, deceitful, and successful lie the devil has influenced people to believe.

Now this scripture is clear and precise and plain enough. And if this was the only one we had to explain this subject it would be enough. But it is by no means the only scripture we have that tells us in no uncertain terms that our responsibility and duty as part of God's creation is to be subject to His authority and to be obedient to His instructed will. Among the many verses that tell us to be subject to God's authority and to obey His commandments is;

1 John 5:2-3.
² by this we know that we love the children of God, when we love God and keep His commandments.
³ for this is the love of God, that we keep His commandments.

God is Serious about Obedience

And just so we can know how serious it really is to be obedient to God's authority, and to know that our salvation depends on it, look at Hebrews 5:9.

⁹ And having been perfected, He became the author of eternal salvation to all who obey Him,

Now this verse gives the positive side and offers eternal life to those who obey God. But there is a negative side as well. Ephesians 5:6 is the negative side and tells what to expect for disobedience.

Ephesians 5:6
⁶ *Let no one deceive you with empty words, for because of these things the wrath of God comes upon the sons of disobedience.*

There are many other scriptures we could quote that show beyond doubt that just like all of God's creation, man is subject to the authority of God and is expected to obey the commandments and instructions found in the word of God, the Bible.

And with all of this evidence and all of these instructions in God's Word, what does this tell us about all of the religious division found in the world today? For one thing, this tells us clearly and without doubt that this religious division is neither authorized nor approved by God.

The churches of Christ have always recognized this and the plea has always been that all those who profess themselves to be Christians and have a desire to submit to the authority of Christ should join themselves together and teach the same doctrines and become part of the one body described in the Word of God. We need to all be of the same mind and be united as one, just as God and Christ are united as one.

Many would ask; how can unity be possible as divided as we are? And this, too, has been considered and studied for many years within the churches of Christ and the answer is much simpler than you might guess.

Why are we divided in the first place?

Don't we all have access to the same Bible? How do we read the Bible and yet have all these different and conflicting doctrines and denominations?

Well, the problem is not with the words within the Bible. The problem is with books and words of men. Different churches and denominations have been starting for 2000 years and new ones are still starting even today. In all these new types of churches their beginning is always the thoughts and desires of one individual.

There are many reasons for starting a new denomination. Some are more sincere than others but all share some things in common. All are rebellious and all promote division and disunity and conflicting doctrines one to another.

And all need some way to show a distinction and difference with other groups. How does one denomination perpetuate their church from one generation to the next and how do they show their members that they are distinct and different from all the others?

All these different denominations do this with a document usually referred to as a creed. This document lays out the statement of beliefs and doctrines that makes this denomination what it is. Without this document the denomination would soon cease to exist. The members would not have the doctrines that designate what makes the group have a separate identity to all the others. Is this beginning to tell you something?

I think most people can readily see that the books and teachings that cause religious division among people who profess to love Christ are not the Bible but are the statements and creeds that are written and intended to highlight and show the differences and the divisions of different denominations. Long ago this was recognized and it was understood that if all religious creeds written by men were discarded and believers in Christ returned to the Bible and only the Bible as the only guide to religious doctrine from God, then denominations would cease to exist. Can you imagine the unity that could be generated if the only book we turned to for instruction in God's word was the Bible? Now, of course we know that this would never be perfect and nothing ever will be. The Bible tells us in;

Matthew 7:13-14;
> [13] *"Enter by the narrow gate; for wide is the gate and broad is the way that leads to destruction, and there are many who go in by it.* [14] *Because narrow is the gate and difficult is the way which leads to life, and there are few who find it.*

Do We Have a Sincere Desire to Submit To the Authority of God?

But do we have a desire to submit to the authority of God? Do we have a desire to be obedient to the will of God? Then what will we do with the words Jesus spoke as His last dying desire for our unity? The plea of the churches of Christ is for unity among those who have a professed reverence for Christianity.

Chapter 3
Do We Have Authority to Change God's Plan

God made a promise to Abraham that he would have a son, and that his descendants would outnumber the stars in the heavens. Abraham believed God and it was accounted to him for righteousness. But as the story plays out in the Bible, God did not say who the mother of this son would be. Look at what the Bible says about this is Genesis 15.

Genesis 15:3-6 (NKJV)
3 Then Abram said, "Look, You have given me no offspring; indeed one born in my house is my heir!"
4 And behold, the word of the Lord came to him, saying, "This one shall not be your heir, but one who will come from your own body shall be your heir."
5 Then He brought him outside and said, "Look now toward heaven, and count the stars if you are able to number them." And He said to him, "So shall your descendants be."
6 And he believed in the Lord, and He accounted it to him for righteousness.

From what we read in the Biblical account we can see that, at first, Sarah, Abraham's wife, seems to feel like she was included in this promise to Abraham. But as time goes on and years pass, Sarah seems to decide that God had not included her in the plan He had for Abraham, and Sarah concludes that she is too old to bear children and not able to give Abraham a son.

Perhaps at this point she had concluded that God was waiting for her to die and for Abraham to remarry and have a son with someone else. We really can't tell what Sarah was thinking and what her true motives were, but for whatever reason, Sarah decided to "help God out with His plan for Abraham".

Most people are familiar with the story of Sarah's attempt to help God produce an offspring for Abraham by giving him Hagar, her Egyptian slave.

Genesis 16:3-4 (NKJV)
3 Then Sarai, Abram's wife, took Hagar her maid, the Egyptian, and gave her to her husband Abram to be his wife, after Abram had dwelt ten years in the land of Canaan.
4 So he went in to Hagar, and she conceived. And when she saw that she had conceived, her mistress became despised in her eyes.

This act was so wrong in so many ways. The ramifications and the consequences of this huge mistake has reverberated down through the ages and changed the course of history in so many ways.

As we know, God had intended for Sarah to have Abraham's son all along. And she did. His name was Isaac and he was the father of many nations and people and was in the linage of Jesus Christ. But Hagar's son, Ishmael, has been the source of strife from the days of Abraham even until today. The religion of Islam owes its existence to the genealogy of Ishmael. Mohammad claims his genealogy through Ishmael.

And that is not the only major thing this mistake cost God's people. There is the problem of multiple wives. The first case recorded in the Bible of a man having multiple wives was the son of the ungodly, rebellious Cain. This account is found in;

Genesis 4:19 (NKJV)
19 Then Lamech took for himself two wives: the name of one was Adah, and the name of the second was Zillah.

There is no mention of any other cases of multiple wives in the Bible until we hear the story of Sarah and Hagar and Abraham. This open door by the father of the Israel nation led to a flood of abuse of God's original plan with Adam and Eve. The plan that Jesus reminded us of when He said,

Matthew 19:4-5 (NKJV)
4 And He answered and said to them, "Have you not read that He who made them at the beginning made them male and female,
5 and said, 'For this reason a man shall leave his father and mother and be joined to his wife, and the two shall become one flesh'?

But the worst thing to happen here is that Sarah tried to help God by designing a plan herself to modify and change the way God already had things designed.

Men have been making this same type of mistake

down through the pages of history and they continue to do it today. It is by this same principle that religions have been designed and created for all these many years and still continues to be designed and created today. We owe the creation of many false religions to the desires of men to "help God out with His design".

But to do this is by no means honorable and acceptable, no more than it was for Sarah to change God's plan. When God's church is redesigned and changed and His religious doctrine is changed into something new, the person who is redesigning has taken on a perceived authority that places him on a higher throne of authority than that of God. Not that the redesigner is usually aware of what he is doing but the consequences are still the same. When this redesigning is carried out and another church comes into existence it has now violated Jesus' final request in the Garden of Gethsemane when He prayed for unity among His followers.

John 17:20-22 (NKJV)
[20] *"I do not pray for these alone, but also for those who will believe in Me through their word;*
[21] *that they all may be one, as You, Father, are in Me, and I in You; that they also may be one in Us, that the world may believe that You sent Me.*

Not only does it violate Jesus' desire in His prayer, it violates God's pattern and plan for the church. The church was never designed to be split and divided into denominations. God has never authorized creating other churches and divisions of the church He designed and created.

The Bible describes the church as "the body". Look at how it is described and designed to stay "one" and undivided.

1 Corinthians 12:13 (NKJV)
13 For by one Spirit we were all baptized into one body--
whether Jews or Greeks, whether slaves or free--
and have all been made to drink into one Spirit.

We have all been baptized into one body, the church. How do we know that the body is the church? The Bible tells us so. We don't have to guess about that part, the Bible is clear. We learn that in many places, but here is one.

Colossians 1:18 (NKJV)
18 And He is the head of the body, the church, who is
the beginning, the firstborn from the dead, that
in all things He may have the preeminence.

So, like God's plan for Abraham to have a son, the church, the body of Christ, is a plan designed by God also. And like Sarah tried to change God's plan for Abraham's son, many people have tried to change God's plan for the church. God does not need or request help to redesign a divine plan. In fact, to do so is sin. We are a part of God's creation and just like all the rest, we are required to submit to the authority of God. If we try to redesign and change God's designs, we enter into an existence where we have no authority to be. We are declaring to ourselves and claiming to have authority that literally overrides the authority of God, Himself.

How do we know what God's plans and designs are for us today?

The answer to that does not come to us through dreams, special revelations or feelings, nor does it come through our emotions. It comes through the study of God's Word, the Bible. The answers are all there but most people never find them, because most people never read what the Bible says. And many people get their religious knowledge in little "sound bites" from other people and then let their emotions and their feelings try to decide what they need to do. This person is easily beguiled and carried away with false teaching.

We need to study for ourselves what the Bible reveals to us. It helps to have a teacher, but everyone must also think and reason for themselves. If you can't read it in the Bible for yourself, don't accept it as fact. Any teacher that helps you must be able to show you in the Holy Scriptures that he is teaching the truth. Good luck to you in your studies.

Chapter 4
Can Truth Contradict Itself?

Is it possible for truth to contradict itself? Think about that. How in the world could it possibly make any logical sense, whatsoever, for two or more versions of "so called truth" openly and notoriously contradict each other......and all be genuine and true ??? And yet this is what we are asked to believe by over 600 religions in the USA alone today. Not to mention all of the others all over the world. No wonder so many people of higher education and intelligence are turned off by religion today. This claim by religious people makes no logical sense what so ever.

Protestant religions today teach differing and contradicting doctrines. This is a fact. And yet they each claim to have the true Gospel of Christ. This is absurd to a logical and intellectual mind. It cannot possibly be and yet it is held up as fact. And what is more absurd is the fact that everyone knows that they contradict one another and every single one of them is celebrated as the true gospel just the same. How in the world can this be?

It wasn't always like this. At least it was not in the Christian's world. Oh, it was in the pagan world and in the world of idolatry. For in these religions they just invented a new god to satisfy their religious thinking and doctrines. But it was not so in the Christian's religion because this religion was designed and delivered by Jesus, Christ, Himself. Jesus designed this church and its beginning is recorded in Bible history in Acts, chapter 2 for all to see.

And it was an impressive and notorious event indeed. It happened in the city of Jerusalem. It was on the day of Pentecost which was a Jewish holiday that occurred 50 days after the Passover. That was 10 days after Jesus ascended up into Heaven.

The Bible describes a mighty sound like hurricane force winds and yet there was no storm. This generated considerable interest in the people of Jerusalem and a huge crowd gathered around to see what was going on. What they saw was even more spectacular. They saw the apostles with flames of fire coming out of their heads. And not only that, when the apostles spoke to the crowd, all of the people from different countries were able to hear the words in their own native language at the same time. That was impressive, to say the least.

And so the church that Christ designed was delivered to the world. A church designed by God. **And guess what...none of the doctrine contradicted itself.** In fact, it was not God's will that this ever change. This fact is recorded everywhere in the Bible. Look at a few passages of scripture and consider what they teach.

John 17:20-21
Neither pray I for these alone, but for them also which shall believe on me through their word;
That they all may be one; as thou, Father, art in me, and I in thee, that they also may be one in us: that the world may believe that thou hast sent me.

These were the words of Jesus, Himself as he prayed for the disciples in the Garden of Gethsemane just before He died.

"That they all may be one"
(as Jesus and God are one.)

And notice who He prayed for.
"All them which shall believe on me through their word." This is all of us who believe on Christ and profess to be Christians. We are to be as united and alike as Jesus and God are united and alike. **This does not mean different and contradicting doctrines, all referred to as "Truth".**
    And look at another scripture.

Gal 1:8-9
8. *but though we, or an angel from heaven, preach any other*
    gospel unto you than that which we have
    preached unto you, let him be accursed.
9. *as we said before, so say I now again, if any man preach*
    any other gospel unto you than that ye have
    received, let him be accursed.

Any other Gospel ????
How many gospels are preached today ???? And this verse includes someone who would claim to receive their gospel by a revelation from an angel. "Let him be accursed". How plain these words are.
    These are but a few of the places warning us not to change the truth of the gospel and to alter the doctrines delivered to us from God. This is serious business and not to be done.
    And yet it is done, and in so many open and notorious cases. How did this ever happen?

And I would say...that the simple answer is.....Rebellion. Ignorance and rebellion are by far the main reasons why the gospel has been altered and changed.

Men hunger for power. Whether it is in the political world or religion, men want power. Within 200 years after Christ established the church, the political world and the church of Christ began to meld together into one false and powerful force. It was not long until the Bible was literally taken out of the hands of the general public and secretly held and guarded by the religious leaders of the time. This went on for many centuries until the true doctrines of the church established by Christ were forgotten by the average man.

This has been referred to as the dark ages by some. This is a true and documented time in the history of our world, noted by almost every "Christian" religion that exists today. The "Clergy" of the time guarded and protected the writings of the Apostles (The Bible) so that only they were able to read what the Bible had to say about the doctrines of the church.

And so, the doctrines were changed...to suit the desires and fancies of those who were corrupted and in charge of the religion of the day. Many others blindly and ignorantly went along with the changes and helped the doctrines to change. Over a period of time and many years, the "church" became so foreign as to be almost unrecognizable to the true church of Christ that was designed and presented to us by God Himself.

And then the printing press was invented.

What an effect this new invention had on the religion of the world. The Bible could be reproduced over and over again and placed into the hands of the average man. It was quite a struggle to be able to do this and live, due to the power of the leaders of the "church" of the day. But it was done...because of the courage of a few. And people began to look and compare...The words of the Bible itself, against the so called doctrines of the then existing church, the Catholic Church. There were so many errors, and so obvious to anyone who could study the Bible for themselves.

And so the reformers began to emerge. Men from everywhere saw the error being taught in the Catholic Church and set out to reform the church and set things right. But they learned quickly that this powerful Catholic Church did not change easily. In fact, it would kill the reformer if it could, and many were executed and killed. Those who were not killed were excommunicated from the church and so they were left to themselves to start a new church with a whole new set of doctrines and rules. And to keep their people together they needed a rule book explaining their teaching of the doctrines of their group so they could be united and alike. And so the "creed" was created.

This happened over and over until more and more groups were formed. And then the groups begin to disagree among themselves and to split apart and more groups were formed. Each with a separate and distinct difference from the others with their own creeds and manuals to keep themselves united together as a separate body. Each one had their own brand of the gospel which they held up as truth. And since they all saw themselves as just a part of the Catholic Church which they thought (in error) was the original church, they called themselves denominations, meaning a fraction or a part of the whole. This went on over and over and year by year until the denominations were so numerous they were almost too many to count.

And eventually, enough was enough.

Several men in different parts of the world began to study the Bible and apply a logical reasoning process to their study and they realized that different and contradicting doctrines were illogical and unreasonable. It was impossible for differing and contradicting doctrines to all be true. They then began to search the Bible for an answer. They studied and realized that the Bible called for all Christians to be united and to teach the same gospel as truth. There was no Bible authority for different gospels and different groups divided by different names. In fact we were commanded to be "one as Jesus and God are one". As they began to try to decide what was dividing these religious groups, it was evident that more importance was being given to the individual creeds than was given to the Bible.

Therein lay a reasonable answer to the problem of the division of the church designed and established by Christ. Since more importance was given to following creeds and disciplines and manuals, and since these writings of men were what spelled out the differences between these denominations, it was logical that these books were a major part of the division. The answer to the problem was to eliminate the books and return to only the Bible as a religious guide for the doctrine of the church. **This was done by many and thus a return to the original church was the plea.** This was not an attempt to reform any existing church but was a plea to **restore the original.** Is this possible you might ask....It sure is. Look at the scripture for the answer.

Luke 8:5
A sower went out to sow his seed:
And his disciples asked him, saying, what might this parable be? Now the parable is this: The seed is the word of God.

The seed is the word of God.........The Bible

If you plant a seed...what develops? If you plant a wheat seed, what do you get? You get wheat. This is a natural law. The words used in religious propagation are from the books used to learn the doctrines. Therefore, the words of the books used are the seed. If you plant a Methodist seed, you get another Methodist. If you plant a Catholic seed, you get another Catholic. If you plant the seed of the words from the doctrine of the original church found in the Bible alone.....You reproduce the church of Christ described in the Bible for all to see. **How could this be wrong???** Any logical reasoning process you bring to this will render the same conclusion...it is a good workable plan.

But people will not give up and abandon their denominations easily. They stubbornly resist change. And many are in positions of power that they would never willingly give up. Not to mention family ties. Many would rather face hell than to give up the church of their dear departed mother or loved one. And so people stubbornly contend that this idea of all doctrines being right even though they contradict one another is reasonable to believe. And they hold on.

And in America and in some parts of the world a **ridiculous explanation of tolerance has been invented.** America was founded on the principal of freedom of religious beliefs. It is reasonable and right to have this freedom and to keep the government from legislating a religion for the state. And we have long taught the idea of tolerance of others who want to practice their religion without persecution. We hold to these principles. But over the years an unreligious liberal element in our country has polluted this idea of tolerance to mean something it was never meant to include.

Tolerance now has taken on a new meaning entirely. Instead of meaning, we accept your right to practice your religion as you see fit without being persecuted, we now are also expected to hold all religions up as credible and equal and "your religion is just as credible and perfectly true as mine". This is the politically correct position people are expected to take. The unlearned and the religiously ignorant and those who are resisting change accept it gladly as though it was somehow valid and correct. May God help us because this makes it 10 times harder to unite the Christians of the land into one church than it would without this false and illogical mindset in our midst.

How about you?

If you have read this far in this material you have an interest in logical things. Can you see that it is the will of God for all Christians to be united into one body? You now know how it can be done. Join the process and help with the struggle. You are needed in the Kingdom of Christ. But before you can be involved in this restoration of the church for others you must be restored yourself. God has chosen preachers to help spread the word to the lost and unlearned.

1 Cor 1:21
21. for after that in the wisdom of God the world by wisdom knew not God, it pleased God by the foolishness of preaching to save them that believe.

If you are not sure what is needed to be restored to the true and original church of Christ that was established by Jesus himself back there 2000 years ago, then seek out a member of the "Church of Christ" and talk with them about it. Do it soon. God needs you and you need God.

Chapter 5
The Old and New Testament

Many people are new to Bible study. And the Bible can sometimes seem complicated and mysterious when a person starts trying to study it for the first time.

So many times people come to a realization that they need to put God in their life and they know that to find knowledge of God and Jesus Christ they must study the Bible. And yet, when they open the Bible for the first time, where and how do you start? Do you start with the beginning of the book? This would be the book of Genesis. It is a long way from the beginning of the book of Genesis to the book of Matthew where we first find the account of Jesus' birth. The entire Old Testament part of the Bible lies in between Genesis and Matthew. And when a person is new to Bible study and knows very little about the divisions of the Bible, this can sometimes cause him to wear out with his study with more questions than answers about God and Jesus Christ. Many times this ends the Bible study with very little information to the person who started out.

The best plan for someone just starting out is to find someone who has the ability to teach the Bible and arrange a Bible study with them to guide you through the difficult beginnings. Once you have the proper divisions of the Bible understood, the Bible begins to make sense when you study. I would suggest you contact a member of the church of

Christ and ask them to recommend a Bible study that you can attend. It would be best if it was just a one on one study where you can be in a relaxed and informal environment where you will feel free to ask questions as they come to mind. The next best thing is to search out a book as a guide to explaining how the Bible is divided into different parts. That is what I intend to do with this chapter in this book.

The Bible itself has something to say about this kind of study. Look at what is said about that.

Romans 10:14 (NKJV)
¹⁴ How then shall they call on Him in whom they have not believed? And how shall they believe in Him of whom they have not heard? And how shall they hear without a preacher?

You can substitute "teacher" for this word "preacher" and it means the same thing. The Bible, itself, tells us that we can benefit from having someone teach us about "Him". And just to show how important it is to properly divide the Bible into its proper order, read what else the Bible says about that.

2 Timothy 2:15 (NKJV)
¹⁵ Be diligent to present yourself approved to God, a worker who does not need to be ashamed, rightly dividing the word of truth.

So we have learned two things so far, to study the Bible we must be able to "rightly divide" it into its proper divisions in order to understand "the word of truth". And the other thing is, that we will benefit if we have a teacher to help us to understand what we read.

There are some things about the division of the Bible that you can teach yourself with the aid of a book such as this. Let's look at just a few.

First off, and most people already know at least a little about this, the Bible is divided into two major divisions; the Old Testament and the New Testament. Sometimes we refer to these sections of the Bible as "the Old Covenant" and "the New Covenant".

The word covenant could be substituted with the word "contract". God has created a contract with the human race. There have been two contracts. There is the old contract, which the Jewish people of the Old Testament were under, and the new contract which we live under today. That is the simple version of the difference between the Old Testament and the New Testament. That is not all there is to it and there is much more to know, but that is the place to start.

For example, this alone explains why we no longer give animal sacrifices today as they did in the Old Testament. Today in the New Testament we no longer have Priests, and animal sacrifices. They are not part of this New Covenant with God. There are many other things that are no longer required in the New Testament. Some of these things are special feast days, circumcision, and all the several hundred laws listed in first 5 books of the Old Testament. Remember, we follow the contract we have with God found in the New Testament and we are not bound and we are no longer following the Old Testament laws.

Colossians 2:14 (NKJV)
^{14} having wiped out the handwriting of requirements that was against us, which was contrary to us. And He has taken it out of the way, having nailed it to the cross.

The Old Testament ended when Christ was crucified on the cross.

But if that is the case, and it is, why then do we even need to study the Old Testament? The Bible answers that question as well.

Romans 15:4 (NKJV)
^{4} For whatever things were written before were written for our learning, that we through the patience and comfort of the Scriptures might have hope.

There are many things to learn found in the Old Testament. It is there that we find the account of the creation of the universe, the earth, and man. We read about the Garden of Eden and the fall of mankind when the woman was tempted and sinned against God. We learn that this great sin caused sin to enter the world and with it came the knowledge of good and evil. Because man was now subject to the moral law, sin passed on to everyone who transgressed these laws. We learn that sin brings eternal separation from God which is spiritual death or eternal hell.

The Old Testament teaches us the eternal consequences of sin and in order to have eternal life we must have redemption from the sin in our lives. The entire Old Testament is an account of the process and the people

God used to Bring Jesus Christ, God's Son, into the earth in order for Him to die for the remission of sin for the lost people of the earth.

The people and events written about in the Old Testament are the direct ancestors of Jesus Christ. We find information about the law they lived under and the way they were required to worship God. We find the way they lived and the battles they fought and the ways they died. We find some who are righteous and some who are evil. We find prophecy after prophecy about the coming of "The Messiah" the savior, Jesus Christ. The Old Testament prepares the way for Christ to come to the earth.

The Old Testament is divided into sections as well. But there are 2 major divisions. These 2 divisions are referred to as "before the great flood" and "after the great flood". Most people know that the people of the earth got so bad within the first 1600 years of man being on the earth that God was almost completely forgotten. Only one man on the earth was righteous in the sight of God. Noah was saved when God instructed him to build the great ark. Noah and his family, a total of 8 people were saved from the flood.

There are also 2 dispensations or "ages" in the Old Testament where God had special ways to govern the people of the earth. From the creation of man until the great flood where the earth was destroyed by water and beyond that to the Great patriarch, Moses, men were governed by God by special revelations to the heads of households. God gave special revelations to the heads of families, or the patriarchs. We can read about God's interaction with these people in the Old Testament.

But when Moses came on the scene, God had a special covenant with him and his people. God created the "Law of Moses" or the "Jewish Law" to govern them.

At this point the patriarchal system changed over to the Jewish Law and the people of God, the Jews, were governed by it until the coming and the death of Christ. We have already read how this Jewish Law system was "nailed to the cross and a new covenant was established for the people of today.

There were 2 types of people on the earth during the Jewish system. There were God's chosen people, the Jews and there were all of the others. The other people were referred to as Gentiles. So during the Old Testament period, there were Jews (sometimes called Israelites) and all the other peoples who were referred to as Gentiles. The Gentiles were governed by the "moral Law", which had governed mankind since the time of Adam and Eve.

Today we are governed by the New Testament. Everything we need to govern ourselves and make us righteous before God is found in the Pages of the New Covenant, the New Contract God has with the people of this earth. Everything we need, to live a good moral life, and everything we need to interact with the people around us, and everything we need to find salvation and eternal life in Heaven with God can be found in the pages of the New Testament. God has preserved for us this book we call The New Testament as our guide for our life on this earth.

This does not mean that we will have good health. This does not mean that we will have happy marriages and good jobs. But if we follow the principals in this book it will go a long way in helping our lives to be happy. Of course there is no guarantee that everything will always be the way we would like for it to be. But it does guarantee that we will be eternally saved and have an everlasting life in Heaven with our God.

So if you are starting a Bible study, perhaps this will help you. But if you have been living a life without God, you have a long way to go. Don't expect that everything bad in your life will just suddenly change for good. It may not. But please don't stop your new commitment to study your Bible and change your life. Every journey starts with a single step.

Chapter 6
The Beginning of the Church

Adam and Eve sinned in the Garden of Eden by eating from the tree of the knowledge of good and evil. Just about everybody knows about this story. But this great sin of Adam and Eve gave all mankind the knowledge of good and evil, and all men became subject to the "moral law". And since no man can obey law perfectly, then all men sinned and became "guilty" of disobedience to God.

This changed God's relationship with man forever. Before Adam and Eve became guilty of sin, God was able to dwell with them and allow them into His presence. After they became guilty of sin, they could no longer dwell in the presence of God. So man became hopelessly lost with no way to redeem himself from the guilt of sin.

Guilt and Death Because of Sin

And the penalty for sin is death, both physical and spiritual. Spiritual death is eternal separation from God and to be cast into "outer darkness where there will be weeping and gnashing of teeth". All of this was the result of Adam's sin in the Garden of Eden.

But from the beginning, God had a plan for mankind to be redeemed. There was no way for man to redeem himself. He could not purchase his redemption because there was nothing that he had that was valuable enough to purchase or redeem his own soul. Of course he could pay the penalty but the penalty was death, eternal separation from God forever.

Christ Had to Die

The only thing that was valuable enough to redeem man was God Himself. This is why Christ had to die on the cross, to redeem us from our sins.

But first man had a lot to learn before he could be redeemed. He had to learn what sin was and why it was so bad. And for the first 4000 years before Christ came to the earth, man was learning about sin and about his relationship with God. From Adam to Noah, and from Noah to Abraham, and from Abraham to Jacob (Israel), God used this time to teach men about their relationship to God and about the severity of sin.

Man Learns About Sin

At first God dealt with the Patriarchs (the heads of the households) and they taught their families. This was the patriarchal age.

God had special relationships with many great men of the Bible. But with Abraham, God made a special contract. He promised Abraham that He would give to him all the land called Canaan, and that through his seed, all the nations of the earth would be blessed. (This was a prophecy of the coming Christ) As a sign of this covenant, all of Abraham's male descendants were to be circumcised.

Abraham's son was named Isaac and Isaac's son was named Jacob, later changed by God to Israel. This was the beginning of the "Children of Israel", the Jews.

Israel had 12 sons who were the 12 tribes of Israel. Because these brothers sold their brother, Joseph, into slavery into Egypt, the Children of Israel spent 430 years as slaves of the Egyptians. God raised up one of their own descendants, Moses, to lead them out of slavery and to the land of Canaan that God had promised their ancestor Abraham many years before.

The Old Contract (Old Law)

God gave Moses the Jewish law for the Jews to obey. There were many rituals and feast days and sacrifices that had to be observed along with washings and purification's, all designed to teach the people about God and sin and what it was all about. The Jews remained under the Jewish law until Christ died on the cross.

The entire Old Testament is a story of the ancestors of Jesus Christ and their lives and their struggles to prepare the way for Jesus to come into the world to redeem mankind from the guilt of our sins.

The story of Jesus begins with the start of the New Testament with the story of His birth.

Jesus started His ministry when He was about 30 years old. When Jesus was 30 years old He chose 12 apostles to help him teach the people and to be witnesses about his ministry and death and resurrection from the dead. Jesus died on the Cross as "a lamb without blemish", a perfect sacrifice for the sins of the world. And not only was His sacrifice valuable enough to save one soul, it was valuable enough to redeem all mankind from their sins, those who were yet to be born, as well as those who had already died.

Not everyone will receive the benefit of Jesus' sacrifice. Only those who are obedient to Gods instructions can benefit from the blood of Christ.

Those people who died before Christ under the Patriarchal system and the Jewish law would receive the benefit of the redemption of Christ's blood too, if they were in favor with God and had been obedient to his Laws when they died.

The New Contract (New Law)

Today we are in the Christian age and not subject to the Jewish law and God has given us a plan of salvation to allow us to be saved with the blood of Christ.

The plan is simple, but notoriously misunderstood.

First we must have faith. We cannot benefit from the sacrifice of Christ unless we believe that He is the Son of God. The Bible is very clear about this and there can be no redemption without faith.

And then there is repentance. Faith without repentance is still of no value. Repentance is more than just being sorry that you have sinned. Of course it includes that but it is more than that, it is also a commitment to change your life and do all you can to live as God would have you live. So, both are necessary to have forgiveness for your sins. Faith and repentance are both required.

But there is more.

We are required to confess that Christ is the son of God. There are cases recorded in the Bible of men who had faith and were not forgiven because they refused to publicly confess that Christ was the Son of God. Either they were afraid for their lives or they were afraid that they would lose their place and status with men if they openly confessed Christ. So the third thing necessary to benefit from the sacrifice of Christ and to receive forgiveness and redemption is to confess that Christ is the Son of God. Many people today will refuse to do that and not be saved for one reason or another.

The next step that the Bible requires in order to be redeemed by the Blood of Christ is baptism for the forgiveness of your sins. There are many counterfeit baptisms, but real baptism is an immersion under water and it is for the purpose of the forgiveness of sin.

There are many false baptisms today. I call them counterfeit baptisms because they are passed off as the real thing and they are very similar. For the uninformed person they look the same, but there is a world of difference.

Some baptisms are by sprinkling or pouring and are not an immersion under water. These baptisms are counterfeit and are not valid or real. Other so called baptisms are not for the remission or forgiveness of sin but are supposed to be a testimony or an example that the person has already had his sins forgiven by some other method, usually by faith alone. Most of the time these people can point to some emotional feeling which they had at the time and associate that emotion with the Holy Spirit and conclude that this was a sign that they were saved. This is not validated by any Bible scripture and is totally against what the Bible has to say about redemption and forgiveness of sin. Some people are baptized as infants and this too is a counterfeit baptism.

To be baptized without faith and repentance and confession that Christ is the Son of God is not to really be baptized at all.

And so, to be able to benefit from the sacrifice of Christ and to be saved by the shedding of His blood will require some obedience on our part as well. We must have faith, we must repent, we must confess that Christ is the Son of God, and we must be baptized for the forgiveness of our sins. When we have done this we still have not earned salvation but we have been saved only by the grace of God which we did nothing to actually deserve. God did it for us because of His love.

God Adds Us to the Church

Once we have been saved, God makes us a part of the Kingdom of Christ. And as we said in the beginning, this kingdom is made up of the people who are saved. We become "sons of God", joint heirs to the everlasting kingdom of Heaven, and able to live in the presence of God forever.

We become children of Abraham, and are as such, God's chosen people. Christ is the head or the king of this kingdom and there is no other head or mediator between God and Man other than Christ himself. We become citizens of this kingdom as those who are "the called out" from the people of the world. We are different from all other people on earth in that we are the saved. We are God's chosen people, the called out, the "ecclesia" or the Church, the body of Christ. The Church is the Kingdom of Christ and it is made up of those who are the saved.

The Church Begins

The beginning of the church is a great story. Right now would be a good time to turn in your Bible to Acts, chapter 2, and read this Biblical account for yourself. It's easy to read and it's easy to understand. You will enjoy the story.

The Church began on the day of Pentecost which was a special feast day to those under the Jewish Law. It was 50 days after Christ had been crucified and had rose from the grave and it was 10 days after He had ascended into heaven to be with God.

Peter preached the first sermon where people were saved by being baptized into Christ. On that day the apostles were gathered together in a room in Jerusalem when a sound of a mighty wind filled the air. And at the same time, tongues of fire were blazing on their heads.

Can you imagine what a spectacular sight this would be to those who saw it? First you hear a mighty hurricane of a wind yet you cannot see the results of a storm. And then these men appear to you with fire on the top of their heads. And not only this, but when they spoke, every one heard what they said in their own native tongues.

There was no doubt to those who saw what was going on but that this was a miraculous event and the source was coming from God. All of this is recorded in Acts, Chapter 2.

When Peter spoke to the people he reminded them that they had just crucified the Christ, the Son of God. And when they realized what they had done, they were "cut to the heart".

You can see the progression of their salvation as you read the account in Acts 2. First they developed faith. This came about through the witness of the miraculous event that was taking place. Then they developed repentance and were "cut to the heart". At this point they ask Peter "what must we do to be saved"? Note that even though they had faith and had repented, they were still not saved as of yet?

There was still another thing they needed to do to receive redemption and to come into contact with the blood of Christ which was able to wash their sins away. And that was to be baptized for the forgiveness of their sins. Note what Peter tells them to do, "Repent and be baptized, every one of you in the name of Jesus Christ for the forgiveness of your sins, and you shall receive the gift of the Holy Spirit". Notice that they were not promised salvation before they were baptized and they were not to receive the Holy Spirit before they were saved? Do you see how important that is?

Some people say that they have received the Holy Spirit before they were saved. They confuse emotion with the indwelling of the Spirit and they credit the experience with salvation without baptism. But you can see by the Bible pattern that this is not how it is done.

In order to be saved you must be baptized first and in Acts 2:47 the Bible says that those who are saved are then added to the Church. In fact it says that, "The Lord added to the Church daily those who were being saved".

Which Church Started?

When Peter preached the first gospel sermon and those who were saved were added to the Church by God, there was no confusion as to which Church they were added to. The reason there was no confusion is because there was only one. That was God's design. There is "One God, one faith, one baptism" and this is the way it was designed by God Himself. The confusion came later and it was caused by man and not by God.

The Church that they were added to was the Kingdom of Christ, those who were called out of the world into God's family by being saved. It had no other name. It was the Church. That was its name. When someone said that they were a member of Christ's Church, everyone knew what that meant. No one said "which Church?" At least not for a long time.

However, it was not long before all of this began to change. Even before the apostles were dead people begin to introduce false doctrine into the Church and lead many astray. Churches were changed and people followed false teaching and false leaders as they have ever since.

Today there are over 600 different religions in the world, each one teaching a different doctrine and all claiming to have the truth and yet their doctrines contradict each other.

This defies all reasonable forms of logic and yet people still try to justify something they don't understand by saying that they are all acceptable to God even though the doctrines they teach are far from the truth God revealed to us in the Bible, and even contradict what he told us to do. No reasonable person can hold this up as truthful logic when he understands what the Bible has to say. However, there may be some people who "have been given a strong delusion to believe a lie" and they may never be able to understand what the Kingdom of Christ is all about.

The Church was quickly perverted and changed by man. This was not God's will and we were warned that it would happen in many places in the Bible. "Men would rise up from among ourselves" who would lead many astray. That is exactly what happened. In less than 300 years the Church was perverted and distorted into a false religion and ceased to be the Church at all.

This did not mean that the Church was gone from off the face of the earth. It was still there and it was still The Kingdom of Christ, but it was not that body that called itself the Catholic Church. That was the perverted kingdom of the Pope, who became a "mediator between God and Man". At least in his eyes he did, but that religion is not the Church which was established by Christ in AD 33. The Church that Paul referred to when he said "The Churches of Christ salutes you" was still on the earth and still made up of those who were added to the Church by God as they were being baptized for the remission of their sins.

The False Church is Not The Original

This new Church, this false Church was structured after the government of the Roman Kingdom. There was the Clergy and the Laity, those in charge and then the regular members.

The Bible says nothing of a Church such as this. We are all "One in Christ", there is neither slave nor free but we are all one in Christ.

Eventually the Clergy removed the Bible from the hands of the people and they were then free to interpret it as they saw fit. Over a thousand years passed before men began to rebel against this false Church effectively.

Once the Bible was translated into the common language many men began to see that something was wrong with the doctrines of this false Church. One by one they sought to reform the Church and one by one they began to start new Churches of their own, held together by another new creed and set of rules which they wrote to tell the members what to believe. Most were similar to the Catholic Church with differences where the gravest of errors in doctrine were seen, but none of which was the Church which was established by Christ. That Church still existed but it was not noticed or recognized as even being there.

Many years later several men began to try to find a way for all Christians to unite and to return to the original Church that was established by Christ in the beginning. They reasoned that if the same things were done today that were done then, we too would be added to that same Church that we read about in the word of God.

We know that the words in the Bible are the seed that produces Christians and it was reasoned that if the pure seed of the word of God is planted in the hearts of men then only Christians would be the result. They realized that the world was full of bad seed. Seed produced by men and not by God. This was in the form of the writings of men that take the place of the pure word of God.

The best way for men to unit was not to try to reform some existing false church but rather to discard all these creeds and manuals written by men and to return to only the Bible as the word to man concerning the Church. If only the Bible is used and followed in its pure and true form then this seed would produce Christians only, who would make up the true original Church, the Kingdom of Christ. This was done and the results were exactly as they expected them to be. The Church of Christ was not reformed by adjusting the doctrines of some other denomination or false Church but by restoring the original Church as it was in the beginning.

But just as in the days of the apostles when they established congregations of the Church and false teachers sprang up and perverted the truth, so it is today. There have been many false teachers who have even invaded the Church of Christ through the years. This invasion always results in false doctrines being introduced and eventually into a split of the members into 2 Churches. The Church of Christ has split many times over the years and many false churches have sprung up which are not the original Church. These are no better than any other false religion and are to be avoided.

The True Seed Produces the Original Church

In order for the Church of Christ to continue as the true original Church of the New Testament it must continue to reproduce itself by the true seed which is the Bible, the pure word of God. There can be no other creeds or manuals. Otherwise the seed is not pure.

The pattern that we have of the true, original Church is found only in the Bible. We must follow the pattern for the Church found there only. Any other pattern would be a Church designed by man and not the true, original Church at all. It is very important that we not deviate from the pattern. To do so is to reconstruct another false Church which is not true to the seed.

It has been over 100 years since the restoration movement began to try to restore the Church to its original form and for many years it was the fastest growing religion in the world. Today, all religion is beginning to lose favor with most of the people of the world, especially in America, and false religions are now growing faster than the Church of Christ. It is no wonder that this is so. People are more educated today and are not so easily beguiled by false religious doctrines that contradict themselves. And because of this, people reject all religion as false.

The religious world has been the big reason why men do not have faith in God. When religions are exposed with different and contradicting doctrines that cannot logically be compatible and all be truth, people consider all religion to be illogical and to be false. This parade of denominations and false churches has turned men's hearts away from God and caused them to consider all religion as false and superstitious myths. What an effective plan the devil has had. Just a few small changes to the Church and a new denomination is created and the seed is no longer pure. After enough time, men's hearts will be turned from God and their morals will then be like a roller coaster ride to Hell. What an effective, subtle plan and we are letting it happen. Perhaps we have very little control.

Nevertheless, it has happened but it is not too late for you. If you are reading this publication then you know what has to be done. Do what you can do to restore the Church that we read about in the Bible; The Church without another name, the "called out", the "ecclesia", the "Kingdom of Christ".

The Pattern for the Original Church

The pattern that is recorded in the Bible of the Church shows that they were baptized for the forgiveness of their sins. But not without faith and repentance and not without confessing that Christ was God's Son. When that was done God added people to the Church, not men. No man puts you into a Church, only God can do this and He only has the one. It is that Church that you become a part of when you are saved.

That Church met together every 1st. day of the week to partake of the Lord's Supper, to sing, to pray, to give as they had been prospered, and to teach God's words to each other through preaching. If we are careful to follow the pattern of this Church as it is revealed to us in the Bible we will only do those things in our worship to God that are revealed to us as a command or by the way of an example or a necessary inference of an act that is revealed.

A necessary inference is an action that is required to carry out a specific command. For instance, if the Bible commands us to sing, we need a song book to carry to this command. The song book would be a "necessary inference", and therefore would also be authorized in the command to sing. We will worship God as he has instructed us to do and not in ways we design ourselves.

It is not good enough for us to devise some form of worship to God that is "not mentioned or criticized" in the Bible. That is not the guide we use to present worship to God. We must only worship God in the ways He has instructed us to do so. Only God knows what worship is acceptable to Him and He has given us instructions in His word as to how we are to do it. Any ways that we design ourselves are not authorized by God and therefore are not a part of the pattern. This would stop us from being true to the seed and we would become "just another false religion" among many.

There are many other things to know and to learn about God's Church, the Church of Christ. You can learn these things by reading the Bible. But most people find this hard to do and the Bible is detailed and very long. It takes years of study to put it all together by yourself and you can easily be led astray by false teachers that you will encounter along the way.

God gave us the Bible but He chose to spread the Gospel through preaching and teaching by men. Find a member of the true Church of Christ and have them help you to study.

This Church will sing in their worship to God as is revealed in the pattern of the Church in the Bible, but like that first true Church, no mechanical instruments will be used.

Musical instruments were used to worship God by the patriarchs and by those under the Jewish Law. But the Church of Christ was told to worship God by singing, the fruit of the lips. Check that out in Eph. 5:19. We are told to speak these songs. And there are many other places where this is repeated. To do anything else in our worship to God is to, once again, design another false Church which is not true to the seed of the word of God.

Many people would say yes, the Bible says to sing by speaking and with the fruit of the lips, but mechanical instruments are not condemned as being wrong so what is the big deal if we add them to our worship? Think about that. Is that the proper way to read and to obey the Bible? When God tells us what to do, is He also supposed to list all the things we are not to do? Is this the way you give instructions? If you were to make a list of things that you needed someone to pick up for you at the grocery store would you also list all the things they were not to pick up? That would not be a logical argument that would allow us to structure God's instructions to suit ourselves. There would be no end to the changes we would make if left up to us to include whatever we wanted to include in God's word just because He did not list it as being a wrong choice. The Bible tells us how to worship God but it never goes into the unlimited ways we could subtly pervert the instructions to do it wrong. But these are unlimited. So to properly follow the teaching and pattern, we do exactly as we are told either by direct command, approved example, or by a necessary inference. (Something that is required in order to carry out a command)

Find a member of the Church of Christ and study this for yourself. May God Bless you in your search.

Chapter 7
The Simple Doctrine of the Church of Christ

I want to give this information in a "matter of fact" format so that these facts can be related to the reader in a space that keeps the thoughts and principles easy to combine together. No doubt, the reader will want to know more about each separate part of this doctrine and that will be a good study to read all you can find about one point at a time. But first, let us explain the total picture in a short enough span to see the overall story.

God created man pure and sinless and free from all the guilt of sin. And because man had no sin, he had a special relationship with God. It was like he lived in Heaven in the presence of God. Everything man needed was supplied for him in the environment where God placed him. This included the tree of life that would allow man to live forever. But there was another tree that existed there as well. It was the tree of the knowledge of good and evil. And God commanded the man not to touch this tree or he would surely die. But you know the story, the woman ate from the tree and she convinced her husband to eat as well. This act was disobedience to the will of God, this was sin. The penalty for this sin had already been set by God, it was death. **And so it happened, that sin entered the world and death because of sin passed to all men.** Don't be confused by this and think that all men are guilty of sin because they have inherited the sin of Adam.

Sin is Disobedience to God

Men are only guilty of sin in their own lives when they disobey God themselves. The thing we inherit from Adam is the knowledge of good and evil. This knowledge passed from Adam to all men. And because we have a knowledge of good and evil, we become subject to the moral laws of God. Children do not have this knowledge when they are too small to understand and so they are not accountable while they are young. But there comes an age when they do understand the difference between right and wrong and when they do wrong they become guilty of sin. And the penalty is still the same for us as it was for Adam.

When Adam and Eve became guilty of sin their world turned upside down. No longer could they be in the presence of God because of their sin. They were banished from the presence of God and driven out of the Garden of Eden. God no longer supplied their every need as though they lived in Heaven. They no longer had access to the tree of life and so they began their physical death that would also pass on to all men. But because they were now guilty of disobedience which was sin, they were already condemned to spiritual death with no hope of being redeemed to their former state with God. A spiritual death is to be forever separated from God.

The question becomes this, what can Adam do to find redemption from eternal spiritual death? Would God just forget this penalty? Or could Adam give God something that would "pay his fine" and eliminate his guilt?

Man's Hopeless Condition

The answer to this is, no. There is nothing that Adam could give to God that God does not already own. Adam, or all of mankind, has nothing valuable enough to give to God that would equal a human life. Perhaps another human life could be substituted in place of ours and pay the price for us. But wait, where would we find someone who would be willing to pay this price for us so we could go free? And if someone would volunteer to do this, where could we find someone who was not guilty of sin themselves and already condemned to death.

The Bible says that "all have sinned and fell short of the glory of God". No, salvation and redemption from the guilt of sin are out of the control of men to save themselves. So what can be done to save man from the penalty and punishment of spiritual death because of sin in our lives? Disobedience leads to sin, and the penalty for all sin is everlasting separation from the presence of God. This is what the Bible refers to as the second death or spiritual death as we refer to it.

But fortunately for us, God understood this problem. And even before the foundations of the earth, God had a solution. There is only one thing that is valuable enough to substitute and pay the price for a man who is condemned to death because of the sin against God. That one thing is God, Himself. And so God became man in the form of Jesus Christ and allowed Himself to die for the redemption of man.

There are very few people in the USA and perhaps even in the entire world who have never heard that salvation and eternal life are found in the Blood of Christ. However, the thing that is elusive and mysterious to those same people in the world is; how do we get into the Blood of Christ so this redemption will cover our sins? The Bible tells us very clearly that all the blessings of salvation are found "in Christ".

Romans 8:1 (NKJV)
¹ there is therefore now no condemnation to those who are in Christ Jesus,

And now that we know where redemption is found, how do we get "in Christ"?

For those of you who have had some association with the various religious groups, you probably have heard common phrases being used that have a familiar sound. Perhaps you have heard the phrase "saved by faith", or maybe you have heard "saved by grace". These phrases are proper and true, but they are almost always misused by all the various denominational churches found on every corner of every street in every town, everywhere. And just in case you haven't figured it out, almost all religion is false. I hate to say that but nevertheless, it is true.

As an example of being saved by grace, suppose someone fell into a river during a heavy flood. That person could likely drown without some type of help. Now just suppose I came along carrying a rope and saw him in the river. Now I could just walk on by and he would likely drown.

But if I had compassion on the person in trouble, I could throw him the rope. Now at this point, this salvation is offered to the person purely because of my grace. He has not done anything for me, and yet I have enough compassion for his condition that I offer him salvation anyway. This is the same way God saves us by His grace. He offers us salvation because He has compassion on our condition and not because we have done anything for Him that would merit His grace.

But just because I offer salvation to this drowning man by throwing him the rope still does not save him. He could just ignore the rope and not take hold to be pulled to safety. It's like that every day with the people of this earth. God offers salvation to every soul alive because of His compassion and grace, but few there be who will "grab the rope" so they can be saved.

We Are Saved By Faith

So as you can see, we are all saved by the grace of God but there is something we have to do as well. What could that part be that we have to do? We will get to that part, but first let's explore the phrase "saved by Faith".

This is a proper phrase as well and the Bible tells us that without faith in Jesus as the Son of God, it will be impossible to please God.

Hebrews 11:6 (NKJV)
⁶ but without faith it is impossible to please Him, for he who comes to God must believe that He is, and that He is a rewarder of those who diligently seek Him.

Faith in Christ is necessary to be saved. The error comes into this teaching when men change this phrase to read that we are saved by "faith only". Now to someone who has not had very much study of the scriptures, this may seem too minor to make a difference. But let me say this; a glass of pure healthy spring water can be rendered a deadly poison by just adding a tiny drop of poison to the glass. I am sorry to have to tell you this but most of the denominational churches teach this very doctrine as God's plan for saving man. They teach this even though the Bible says clearly;

James 2:24 (NKJV)
[24] *You see then that a man is justified by works, and not by faith only.*

Grace, Faith, and "In Christ Jesus"

So now we have discovered three things about salvation. We are saved by God's grace, we are saved when we find our way to be "in Christ" and we are saved by "faith in Jesus Christ". And you may have noticed in the passage in James that we are also saved by "works". A study of the Bible would reveal that the word works as used here is referring to "obedience to God's instructions". And just as Jesus' brother, James tells us in James 2: 24, we cannot be saved without obedience to God's instructions.

What are the instructions that God has given us concerning being saved? We have already discovered that to find the benefits of salvation one has to be "in Christ". So what are God's requirements to be in Christ?

We know that faith in Christ is required, but what else? And suppose we do find that the Bible tells us that we are required to do something to be saved?

What then?

Would that really be convincing enough to cause someone who is biased with years of error in a religious doctrine to change their mind? Usually it is not enough. Before the teaching of the Bible can find a place in the hearts of men and begin to grow in fertile ground, the heart must be unbiased and open to receive it. Turning loose of old false doctrine that has been accepted for years, is more than many can do. For you see, it is just not a desire to serve God that keeps men in false religions, it is a connection to family, friends, and comfort. But for those who have no such biased connections, let's look at what God tells us to do to be saved.

To be saved, a person must hear the Gospel. The Gospel is nothing more than the message of salvation. But the Bible declares that the power to be saved comes to us that way. It will not come in some miraculous vision or some emotional feeling that is better felt than told. It will come by hearing the words from God that are revealed to us by the Holy Spirit and are written in the Bible. Look at what the Bible has to say about that.

Romans 1:16 (NKJV)
^{16} For I am not ashamed of the gospel of Christ, for it is the power of God to salvation for everyone who believes, for the Jew first and also for the Greek.

And Again:
Romans 10:14 (NKJV)
¹⁴ How then shall they call on Him in whom they have not believed? And how shall they believe in Him of whom they have not heard? And how shall they hear without a preacher?

So the process that takes us to salvation is the Gospel. And we find this Gospel by hearing it proclaimed or preached or taught to us by a teacher. It does not come in dreams and it does not come through emotional feelings. It comes by hearing the word of God taught from the Bible.

This Gospel of salvation includes certain things that God tells us to do. One of which is to "confess His name before men". Why do you suppose that would be so important that it is required for salvation? The Bible declares to us that we cannot be saved without it. Let's look at what the Bible says about this.

What is the Gospel of Salvation?
Is Confession Required?
What is Confession?

Romans 10:9-10 (NKJV)
⁹ that if you confess with your mouth the Lord Jesus and believe in your heart that God has raised Him from the dead, you will be saved.
¹⁰ For with the heart one believes unto righteousness, and with the mouth confession is made unto salvation.

Look carefully at what these scriptures say. Do you see that it says "if you confess with your mouth" you will be saved? What will be the condition of those who do not confess Christ? No one really has to tell you that. The Bible explains itself in these verses found here. But just in case this is not enough;

John 12:42-43 (NKJV)
⁴² nevertheless even among the rulers many believed in Him, but because of the Pharisees they did not confess Him, lest they should be put out of the synagogue;
⁴³ for they loved the praise of men more than the praise of God.

There are many reasons why men will refuse to confess Christ as God's Son and the Lord of their lives. If anyone has a reason that would keep them from confessing Christ in a public way, they will not be saved.

Is Faith "Only" in the Bible?

But what if someone wants to do these things but refuses to change their life and turn from their sinful ways. Suppose a person has a great faith in God and Christ and has no doubt that Jesus is the Son of God and suppose he is willing to confess publicly that Jesus is the Son of God. Would this be enough to for him to be saved? There are hundreds of people in denominations all over the world who proclaim loudly that the only thing required for salvation is "faith alone". That sounds good and it is preached everywhere, but is it true? Is faith really enough, alone?

Once again, look at what the Bible has to say. The Bible has plenty to say about faith alone and it is clear that the message of the saving Gospel is more than faith alone. If faith alone will save anyone, then the devil is saved.

James 2:19-20 (NKJV)
19 You believe that there is one God. You do well. Even the demons believe--and tremble!
20 But do you want to know, O foolish man, that faith without works is dead?

It's pretty clear that the devil has faith. But is the devil saved? Of course he is not? It takes more than faith to be saved. The devil has faith "alone" but he lacks those other things referred to here as "works" or as we have said before, "obedience".

Repentance for Salvation

Do you think the devil would be willing to repent of his sins? I think we know the answer to that, he would not. But the Bible says it is required for salvation. We have to be willing to change our life. We must repent of the sins in our life and make a change to turn away from anything that the Bible considers sin. There are many places in the Bible where we are told to do this in order to be saved.

Acts 3:19 (NKJV)
19 Repent therefore and be converted, that your sins may be blotted out,

Luke 13:3 (NKJV)
2 And Jesus answered and said to them,
3 I tell you, no; but unless you repent you will all likewise perish.

Would it really make any sense for a person to think God would save him if he had no intention of changing his sinful ways? It was sin that caused him to need salvation in the first place. How would it make any sense to claim to be a disciple of Jesus Christ and live a life of contemptible sin? I do understand that it would be very hard to live a life and never, ever sin even after a person is saved. But there is a big difference in trying to "walk in the light" and being free from a life of sin and not even trying to repent and live a life for God. The Bible has something to say about this as well.

1 John 1:6-9 (NKJV)
⁶ If we say that we have fellowship with Him, and walk
in darkness, we lie and do not practice the truth.
⁷ But if we walk in the light as He is in the light, we have
fellowship with one another, and the blood of
Jesus Christ His Son cleanses us from all sin.
⁸ If we say that we have no sin, we deceive ourselves,
and the truth is not in us.
⁹ If we confess our sins, He is faithful and just to forgive
us our sins and to cleanse us from all
unrighteousness.

Look at verse 7. If we are striving to be obedient to God, and we are walking in the light, the blood of Jesus Christ forgives us of all sin. But let us not lose sight of the requirements for this to happen. The requirement is that there is a sincere effort taking place to walk in the light. There is a caution in the scriptures about trying to take advantage of this blood and continuing to sin after we are saved.

Romans 6:1-2 (NKJV)
¹ What shall we say then? Shall we continue in sin that grace may abound?
² Certainly not! How shall we who died to sin live any longer in it?

So there is the caution. If anyone disregards God's caution and does not walk in the light, they cannot expect to be saved.

Baptism is for Forgivness

So now we have discovered that we are saved by God's grace, when we hear about Christ and develop a faith in Him that causes us to "obey the Gospel". And by obeying the Gospel we now understand that we are instructed to repent of our sins and publicly confess Christ as God's Son.

If you have read this far you are beginning to understand what it means to "obey the Gospel".

There is still another requirement to be saved. You have not obeyed the Gospel until you have completely followed God's plan of salvation as He has designed it and revealed it to us in His Holy Word, the Bible.

There is "baptism for the remission of sins".

Denominational churches fight this requirement with all the false teaching they can muster. They have to. For you see, if this part of the Gospel plan of salvation is true, then their entire system of religion is proved to be false. They teach salvation by "faith alone". But even without knowing about baptism for the forgiveness of sins, you have already learned that this doctrine is untrue. We have just read that the Bible declares *"the demons believe and tremble"*.

But what does the Bible tell us about the purpose of baptism? Look at some of the scriptures about this.

Acts 2:37-39 (NKJV)
^{37} Now when they heard this, they were cut to the heart, and said to Peter and the rest of the apostles, "Men and brethren, what shall we do?"
^{38} Then Peter said to them, "Repent, and let every one of you be baptized in the name of Jesus Christ for the remission of sins; and you shall receive the gift of the Holy Spirit.
^{39} For the promise is to you and to your children, and to all who are afar off, as many as the Lord our God will call."

Here is a case where the men who crucified Christ had suddenly realized that they had sinned and needed salvation. They asked Peter what they should do. Peter's answer was simple. In one sense, he said "obey the Gospel". But the words said this; "repent and be baptized" for the remission of your sins. Yes, read this one more time. He said repentance and baptism are for forgiveness of sins.

Now we read this together and we read it straight out of the Bible and it is very clear. How could anyone misinterpret this message? They could not, that is, unless there was a great desire to do so because of other reasons. But in case this is just not enough, there is more. There is much more.

There are many, many scriptures telling us that baptism is for the forgiveness of sins.

Acts 22:16 (NKJV)
^{16}And now why are you waiting? Arise and be baptized, and wash away your sins, calling on the name of the Lord.'

These are the words said to Saul, who later was called the Apostle Paul, after he saw and spoke to Jesus on the road to Damascus. Saul had developed a sincere faith in Christ when Jesus struck him blind and Saul also confessed Christ as Lord and the Son of God. There is also no doubt that Saul repented of his sins when this happened to him. But Saul had not completely obeyed the Gospel until he was baptized to "wash away his sins".

There are many other passages we could quote but this is enough to get the message across to anyone whose heart is fertile ground for the Gospel to take root and to grow and produce fruit. The question will now be; Will you be one who finds the "narrow gate" and is saved or will you be among the majority who find the broad way to destruction?

I have attempted to explain the Gospel plan of salvation in simple terms that I hope and pray are easy to understand. If this is not clear enough or if you now have a hunger and thirst to know more, attend the church of Christ or call one on the phone and I assure you that whoever you ask will be happy and willing to teach you more about these things I have written about, and more.

Just to make this clear, the Gospel plan of salvation is simple and plain. There are 5 steps that are simple for all men to understand.

The 5 Steps of Salvation

These 5 steps are given to us by the grace of God, so that all men may be saved.
1. Hear the Gospel,
2. Believe on the Lord Jesus Christ
3. Repent of your sins,
4. Confess publicly that Jesus is God's Son,
5. Be baptized by immersion for the forgiveness of sins.

These are the 5 simple steps that make up the Gospel plan of salvation.

Chapter 8
Born Again

If you are new to Bible study you probably have already heard the term *"born again"*. You might not have a full understanding of what this phrase actually means, but don't fret. Very few people, even those who think they are religious, don't really understand it. Even those who think they do. So let's look at this term and see how the Bible defines what it means. Let's look at the Bible verse where we see this analogy used in the Scriptures.

John 3:3-5 (NKJV)
³ Jesus answered and said to him, "Most assuredly, I say to you, unless one is born again, he cannot see the kingdom of God."
⁴ Nicodemus said to Him, "How can a man be born when he is old? Can he enter a second time into his mother's womb and be born?"
⁵ Jesus answered, "Most assuredly, I say to you, unless one is born of water and the Spirit, he cannot enter the kingdom of God.

So what do we see here first thing in verse 3?
Verse 3 tells us that being "born again" is absolutely necessary in order for a person to be saved. Without it "you cannot see the "kingdom of God". So that alone tells us that we need to understand what this is. We can tell by verse 4 that this is not the natural birth that Jesus is referring to here. No one can enter into their mother's womb and be

born again that way. This has another meaning other than that.

Verse 5 makes this so simple and so obvious that in order to misunderstand this process you actually need a false teacher to spin it in such a way that it confuses the issue. And rest assured; men have been doing this for centuries.

Jesus Says "Born of Water"

Look at how Jesus answers Nicodemus in verse 5. He says, *"Unless one is born of water and the Spirit, he cannot enter the kingdom of God."* Notice here that the word Spirit is capitalized? This word is referring to the Holy Spirit of God. And does the word "water" really present any problem in our understanding of these verses? This is an obvious reference to baptism.

We have already discussed in another chapter of this book that baptism is one of the five steps to salvation and we have shown baptism to be part of the Gospel plan of salvation. But to review, look again at Acts 2:38.

Acts 2:38-39 (NKJV)
[38] Then Peter said to them, "Repent, and let every one of you be baptized in the name of Jesus Christ for the remission of sins; and you shall receive the gift of the Holy Spirit.
[39] For the promise is to you and to your children, and to all who are afar off, as many as the Lord our God will call."

And if That is Not Enough

Mark 16:15-16 (NKJV)
15 And He said to them, "Go into all the world and preach the gospel to every creature.
16 He who believes and is baptized will be saved; but he who does not believe will be condemned.

There are many more Scriptures that can be quoted to show that baptism is a part of God's Gospel plan of salvation and is required to be saved. Jesus is giving this same information to Nicodemus.

There are 2 parts to the salvation process. There is the part we do and there is the part that God does for us. Our part is to hear, believe, repent, confess, and be baptized. God's part is Spiritual. God changes our lives from the old sinful man that is spiritually dead in sin to a brand new man who is spiritually new and sin free.

This process of changing to a "new person" is explained for us in Romans 6.

.
Romans 6:2-4 (NKJV)
2 Certainly not! How shall we who died to sin live any longer in it?
3 Or do you not know that as many of us as were baptized into Christ Jesus were baptized into His death?
4 Therefore we were buried with Him through baptism into death, that just as Christ was raised from the dead by the glory of the Father, even so we also should walk in newness of life.

So there is a "new birth" when we are *"baptized into His death"*.

We are raise from the dead by the *"glory of the Father, even so we also should walk in newness of life."*

In other words, **"we are born again"**. There is the physical part and there is the Spiritual part. When Jesus said to Nicodemus that we must be born again by water and Spirit, this is exactly what He meant.

Do we need to be born again? Now you know the answer to that question. From now on, if someone tells you that you need this, you will probably know more about what it means than the person who mentioned it.

You are Now The Teacher of This

The reason you will know more about what this means than the person who said it to you is because for hundreds of years, beginning with the Catholic church, men have preached a false and appealing doctrine of "salvation by faith alone". Now if you were teaching a doctrine such as this, what in the world would you do with these statements Jesus made to Nicodemus? As you can see they are not hard at all to understand, but they just totally fly in the face of anyone who would deny that baptism is part of the salvation process. So if you were trying to defend a false doctrine that said you are saved by "faith alone" and baptism is not required to be saved, how would you get around what Jesus said to Nicodemus? Well, they do it in quite a ridiculous way and yet at the same time quite ingenious, too.

Many will say that being born again in the Spirit is God's Spiritual part of the saving process.

They would actually be right if they actually meant this as we just described it, but unfortunately they usually have other meanings when they say that part too. But it is the water part that really gives them the trouble. Since the doctrine of "faith only" leaves no room for baptism, they have to give it some other meaning. And the meaning chosen is to say that being born of water is the natural birth when a baby comes into this world and water is a part of the natural birth process. I don't really have to tell you that this is not what these verses are referring to. The first part of this explanation brought the proper meaning to light. The proper meaning of born again is too simple to misunderstand unless you have someone to help it become confusing.

Chapter 9
What about Repentance Are All Sins Equal?

  I hesitated about including this topic in this book. But if you are reading this, there is a very good possibility that you are considering making some very important changes in your life. I hope that you came into possession of this book because someone gave it to you. That's the reason the book exists and I hope you will consider passing it on to someone else when you have finished with it.

  Are you searching for something? Is there something in your life that you feel like you want to change? Have you considered that there is a way to live our lives that God approves? If this is the case for you, then you already know that there are changes in your life that you need to make. This change is called repentance, and it is not just an option, it is required.

  There are so many people today who are searching for a more meaningful existence, hoping to find it through some "mysterious" connection to God through some religious connection. And in today's moral climate and cultural decay, a "politically correct" world view usually includes one foot in religion and one foot still planted in a familiar world of "acceptable sin". But if you really want a more meaningful existence, it won't be found that way.

  Through the years as I have lived, I have personally watched the world redefine the meaning of sin.

Things that once were considered grievous sins have today been redefined as acceptable behaviors in life. In my lifetime I have saw the evil, sinful behavior of homosexual activity brought from hiding in the shadows of darkness and black corners to publicly celebrated and honored in the light. And I have seen pornography displayed as acceptable and fornication publically flaunted in the face of anyone who might object, even to the point of destroying the marriage of men and women and driving a stake in the heart of the family unit. Sin has been successfully redefined in the eyes of the people of this world. Do you want to change your life? Then repentance is not an option, it is required.

Sometimes people who see the need for religion in their lives have a misconception of the true meaning of repentance. Many times their understanding and definition of repentance is being sorrowful about their past life. There is some truth to that understanding but that definition is by no means complete. There is more to repentance than just being sorrowful for our past life. In addition to that, there must be a dedication and commitment to renounce sin and live a clean and sin free life. Have you been caught up in some sin? Even if the world considers it acceptable according to the world's definition of sin, repentance requires you to renounce and eliminate this sin from your presence. You cannot claim repentance with one foot still involved in the presence of sin.

Remember this; sinful behavior is the religion of Satan. Would it seem reasonable to be a member of God's church and practice the religion of Satan at the same time?

Think about that. Would it really be honorable to try to continue in sin after we are "born again"? Could we really expect to still have God's blessings and grace if we do not repent? Look at what the Bible has to say about this.

Romans 6:1-4 (NKJV)
¹ What shall we say then? Shall we continue in sin that grace may abound?
² Certainly not! How shall we who died to sin live any longer in it?
³ Or do you not know that as many of us as were baptized into Christ Jesus were baptized into His death?
⁴ Therefore we were buried with Him through baptism into death, that just as Christ was raised from the dead by the glory of the Father, even so we also should walk in newness of life.

"We are raised to walk in newness of life". What wonderful words these are for those hopelessly lost in sin. God has given us a way to totally destroy the old man of sin and be reborn into a world as a brand new person and clean and free from all of our past sinful life. This is the greatest of second chances and it is free and available for all those who will obey God and receive it. And men do receive it.

But it is very hard and perhaps even impossible for a person to live a life completely free of sin, even after they have been born again and forgiven of the past sins in their life. The Bible tells us that everyone sins and has a need for forgiveness and redemption in order to have eternal salvation with God. We know that we find this salvation through faith in Jesus Christ as God's Son and by obedience to the "Gospel plan of salvation".

This plan is faith, repentance, confession, and baptism for the forgiveness of our sins. We can read about this sin in;

Romans 3:23-24 (NKJV)
[23] *for all have sinned and fall short of the glory of God,*
[24] *being justified freely by His grace through the redemption that is in Christ Jesus,*

Do you notice that this says that all "have sinned" and are justified through the redemption that is in Jesus Christ? What it does not say is that all "are sinning" and being justified by Jesus Christ. Just the opposite is taught in the verse we quoted in Romans. Let's look at that verse again.

Romans 6:1-4 (NKJV)
[1] *What shall we say then? Shall we continue in sin that grace may abound?*

The Bible's position on this is clear. We are forgiven of past sins when we obey the Gospel but we are to renounce sin and repent and we are not to be associated with it again. In fact we are to live our lives as examples to encourage the rest of the world to imitate us as we live a Christian life.

But in spite of this commitment and resolve, we could slip up and sin anyway. Being human it is very hard to live a totally sin free life and God has given us a provision in case that should happen.

1 John 1:7-9 (NKJV)
[7] *But if we walk in the light as He is in the light, we have fellowship with one another, and the blood of*

> *Jesus Christ His Son cleanses us from all sin.*
> *⁸ If we say that we have no sin, we deceive ourselves, and the truth is not in us.*
> *⁹ If we confess our sins, He is faithful and just to forgive us our sins and to cleanse us from all unrighteousness.*

This is a provision in case we sin after we have been born again. But this is not to be uses as a "crutch" and given great sweeping power to blot out sin. That would make being a Christian cheap and unrespectable. Notice what is said by the text. First off, it is referring to those who "walk in the light". Who are those people? We know who they are. These are the people who are walking in the light as "He is in the light". These are the people who are trying their best to live their lives as Jesus asked them to live. These are not people who intend to sin. These are those who have repented and turned away from even the appearance of sin. These are Christian people who "slip up". And notice what the text says about "confessing our sins". Yes, God will forgive us if we sin, providing we are really living our life "in the light".

But the real reason I am writing this chapter is because people don't have the same understanding of the hurtful, grievous nature of sin as it is defined and described in the Bible definition. This is because a complete generation has now grown up in a world where sin has been redefined.

As an example, I am seeing homosexuality being addressed more and more in "Christian" environments as an acceptable alternate lifestyle which some people just seem to "mysteriously" possess. This softening of the "Christian" position for the homosexual has developed because of a cultural change within the world around us. Some religions and some denominations just follow the lead of the culture of society and do not condemn homosexual behavior at all. Some will even accept the homosexual lifestyle into full fellowship of their church. Others will make some distinction between the homosexual behaviors but will welcome the homosexual and allow him to continue to openly call attention to his life as a so called celibate homosexual. Some even have open discussions with homosexuals who see themselves as homosexuals, but are trying not to participate in an active homosexual life style. These people are not asked to fully renounce the homosexual life as sinful and repugnant but are just asked not to participate in homosexual fornication. This sends a very destructive message to other people especially to youth in the church. This is usually done by tender hearted people who just want to "include" and "nurture" everyone who has a need. I heard of a man once who had teenage daughters at home and he felt a need to "rescue" homeless and troubled boys and bring them home to let them live with his family. Do I have to tell you what the end result of this was?

Some people justify this "gentleness" with the homosexual on the grounds that "we all sin" and "all forms of sin are equal". So because no one sin is worse than another, any sinner who says he repents should be allowed complete and open fellowship with the congregation with no regard for any temptations, tendencies, image or lifestyle they present or represent. This does not make good common sense. What would you expect to do with a pedophile who says he repents? Would you send him to a church Bible camp as a councelor for your children? Surely not! We know that people can be forgiven for any sin, but that does not stop us from using good common sense when we deal with these people in our midst.

All sin is not the same and all sin is not equal. Many times people quote this passage to try to prove all sin is equal.

James 2:10 (NKJV)
¹⁰ for whoever shall keep the whole law, and yet stumble in one point, he is guilty of all.

If you read the entire chapter here you will discover that James is referring to people who were giving respect and honor to rich people and giving dishonor to the poor. He points out that we cannot ignore parts of the law and give respect to other parts. All the law is important. This includes the law of Christ. But this is not saying that all sin is equal. A quick check of common sense reasoning will tell us this point is true.

If we use the Old Testament as a guide to this test, then consider the legal punishment for certain sins described in the Old Testament Law. Some sins were so severe that those found guilty were given the death penalty and yet there were other sins where the legal penalty was not so severe.

And in the New Testament we can read the words of Jesus Himself when he said to Pilot;

John 19:11 (NKJV)
^{11} Jesus answered, "You could have no power at all against Me unless it had been given you from above. Therefore the one who delivered Me to you has the greater sin."

Notice here that Jesus refers to a "greater sin"? There are many places we can turn to in the Bible that also reveal this concept, but I would like to point out the Old Testament story of Sodom and Gomorra and the total destruction of these cities because of the terrible sin of the homosexual people of these cities. Most people are familiar with this story found in Genesis 18;

Genesis 18:20 (NKJV)
^{20} And the Lord said, "Because the outcry against Sodom and Gomorrah is great, and because their sin is very grave,

God described their sin of homosexuality as grave.

Now the reason I brought all this up is to point out the seriousness of repentance and to remind us all that to repent of sin is to renounce and reject the entire concept of the image of sin in our lives. There is no such thing as repentance with strings attached to the old sinful life. Not for homosexuality, not for adultery, not for lying, not for pedophilia, and not for anything. And be prepared to eliminate the very image and everything connected to any past sins when you are "born again". Repentance is a serious thing and there can be no redemption and justification without it. Repentance is just as important as faith, confession and baptism for the forgiveness of our sins. Sometimes people get "fixated" on faith and forget repentance, confession and baptism. And sometimes people get fixated on baptism and forget the importance of repentance, confession and faith. A "partial Gospel" is not a saving Gospel. It takes the entire Gospel plan of salvation for us to be saved.

PAST SINS
Carl O. Cooper

The sins of the past, although forgiven,
Are fences and scars
On our journey to heaven.

Do not allow sin to hold any fame.
But to hide in a closet
In repentance and shame.

For Satan will test you and tempt you with pride.
By recalling the sins
Of that old life that died.

For the new life you live should be seen and esteemed,
And your friends and your brothers
Should know you're redeemed.

Brothers, don't bring up your old sins even to teach others a point.
Don't mention them
Don't use yourself as a teaching example.

Chapter 10
Fundamental principles in the church of Christ

The Church of Christ differs from all other religious groups in existence in the fundamental foundation of hermeneutic principles on which the doctrine of the church is determined. Why do we believe what we believe, and why do we do what we do in our worship to God? The answers to these questions are so vitally important that to misunderstand and to misapply is to degrade the Church to "just another denominational faction", among the many.

The solid foundation footing on which the whole church's doctrine concerning worship to God rests is on the principle that in doctrine **"we speak where the Bible speaks and are silent where the Bible is silent"**. By this we mean that we are free to teach and to do those things in our worship to God **"that are authorized by the Bible"** and we are not free to do those things that are not. The very fact that some things are *not specifically condemned* is enough to allow them to be practiced in almost all denominational religions. This is not the case in The Church of Christ and is the basic foundation principle on which the very existence of the Church rests.

There is revealed in the Bible a true system of religion. It is designed by God and it reflects his will in all matters of religious belief and in worship to Him. God, Himself, has told us what is acceptable and has revealed to us a pattern and an identity. The acts of worship to God are revealed to us as well as a pattern for God's church which is identified as *"The Bride of Christ"*. This pattern for the Church, this system of "Faith" is revealed and spread by means of the word of God, the Bible, which is referred to as "The seed". When this seed, this pattern, is planted in the hearts of men, this system of religion springs forth and is reborn and begins to reproduce another identical duplicate. This will happen over and over as long as the true seed finds roots in the pure hearts of men. *There is a problem when the seed is altered.* If the seed is altered, then the plant that springs forth is no longer identical to the original. And this is the cause for the religious division that is so common within our world today. Every time an altered seed is planted in the mind and heart of a believer the seed takes root and a new plant is born. The new plant is a mutant and is not true to the original form. In order to have the true plant, the original form, only the true original seed can be planted. This is why it is absolutely necessary that we hold fast to the foundation footing on which the pattern of the Church rests.

One of the ways in which the *Bible teaches us is with "commands"*. Very few people would dispute the fact that when the Bible gives us a command it is to be obeyed. And so there is usually agreement among religious people that we obey what God tells us to do as a command. There is a basic principal on which common sense and logic tells us how to obey a command. But it is here where the lines are drawn and the seed becomes altered. A command that authorizes things will at the same time disallow things with the same statement and the same few words. For instance, if your employer sent you to the supply house to purchase copy paper, then you are authorized to purchase copy paper. And although he did not give you a list of all the many other things you are not to purchase, those things are automatically disallowed. This is the *"law of inclusion and exclusion."* The command includes what is necessary to carry out the command but at the same time excludes those things that are not. Many people do not see this distinction in religious commands and so they feel justified in doing anything in religion that has not been specifically condemned. It is at this point that the seed becomes altered.

There are many examples that one could use to show this connection, but a common one is *the use of instruments in worship to God.* The Bible is clear in the command. No one disputes that the Bible commands us to sing in our worship to God. And in many places the words "sing", "fruit of the lips", "Psalms, hymns, and spiritual songs" are used to designate singing as a means to worship God. No one disputes this as far as I know. But the Bible does not list the many other things that could take the place of singing. Playing musical instruments is one, dancing is another, and we could list many more. Burning candles or incense, playing music to meditate by, flashing lights, and choirs are just a few of the ways men have chosen to try to add worship to God in a way He has not specified. These things are done on the basis that the Bible does not specifically forbid them. *But the law of inclusion and exclusion rules them out.*

Many people are **drawn to religion because of a**

connection to music which I personally as of yet do not understand. I know that *there is a mysterious connection and link* and I hope to someday have a better understanding as to what this is. Music is a major factor in many people's lives. In some cases because of a talent they possess to play instruments or to sing and perhaps because of the feelings they get when they are exposed to music and musical instruments. Religion is a place where these talents or these feelings can be exercised and ignited in a way that brings fulfillment to the person who possesses them. There is a genuine love for musical instruments in a great number of people who are involved in the Church. The temptation and the draw toward using instruments in worship to God is exceptionally great. **Why would God not love and want what they want and love so well?**

Many people give up a lot to come into the Church of Christ. But this is one area where they are tested in their commitment to genuine obedience to God. *Perhaps this is why God left the instruments out of the pattern for the Church.* The lack of musical instruments in worship could be a test to determine genuine commitment to His will. In many cases people do leave the instrument out of their worship to God and go on to become more and more committed to the foundation principles on which the Church is based. But in some cases the desire is too strong and although they seem to have left the instrument behind it is still with them and merely suppressed for a time until the opportunity presents itself to become a stumbling block for themselves and the rest of the Church as well. *As time goes on I find that there are more and more of these types of people within the Church.* They go unnoticed for a long time until the numbers multiply. When they are of sufficient numbers to notice each other a problem begins to develop within the Church. It is subtle at first but as numbers increase and the people who are like minded become more open and vocal in their opinion, the mood of the congregation begins to shift. Unless those in leadership capacity are courageous and strong, the congregation can be overtaken in this sin. Considering that there is already a great number within the Church who have been attracted to religion because of the **mysterious connection of the "music/religion link"** there is no shortage of people in whom there is a desire for the instrument to be used. In most people it is forever suppressed, but if a leader emerges they can be sorely tempted to go along with the crowd.

    This is a plea to be committed to the foundation principles of the Church of Christ, and to be committed to planting the pure and unaltered seed of the Word of God, and to speak where the Bible speaks and to be silent where the Bible is silent. To be ready and willing to obey every command revealed by God as to how we are to worship Him and to *never, never add anything to our worship just because we have reasoned that it is not specifically condemned.* I am worried that we are beginning to find ourselves in less and less a majority in the Churches of Christ who are committed to these basic restoration principles. We need to begin now with a renewed effort to teach these basic doctrines to our congregations and our young people everywhere. Unless these basic doctrinal principles are renewed in the hearts and minds of our people soon, they will be lost in the generations to come. Some will not be able to bear it and will abandon us and this will not be our desire, but it is better to lose a hand than an entire body. **In the long run people will be attracted to a movement that has commitment to a rock solid foundation** where there is stability of logic and common sense and where the **people genuinely practice something in which they really believe,** *even if and especially if it separates them from the rest of the religious world.*

Chapter 11
Instrumental music in the church

Have you ever considered why we worship on the first day of the week? Why not on the Sabbath like the Jews? After all, the Jews worshipped God on Saturday for thousands of years before Jesus came to this earth. Why would God suddenly change the day Christians were to worship and make it a different day than the Jews had always observed? Doesn't the answer seem obvious when you consider the question for a minute or two? God fully intended to present to the world a new and different religion. God presented to the world a complete new covenant with a whole new design. There were no more requirements to make sacrifices and keep feast days. It was no longer a requirement to be circumcised or to keep the Jewish Law. God knew that men would have a hard time adjusting to this new religion and it would have been much harder to adjust if the two religions were so much alike that it was hard to tell them apart. So God created and designed into the Christian religion special changes that showed, without a doubt, that these religions were not the same. Changing the day on which the people assembled to worship was one of the changes that God designed. But there were others.

Another great change was in the worship which God designed and authorized to be offered and presented to Him. The old ways men worshipped God were not incorporated into this new design. There were many changes in the new design for worship, but the one I would like to focus on here is the use of musical instruments when we worship God. It was a common part of the worship to God in the Old Testament to worship Him using musical instruments. There are many Old Testament scriptures we could quote to show their common use.

2 Samuel 6:5 (NKJV)
⁵ Then David and all the house of Israel played music before the Lord on all kinds of instruments of fir wood, on harps, on stringed instruments, on tambourines, on sistrums, and on cymbals.

But this is not the case for the worship God designed for the Christian age. You can search the New Testament from Matthew to Revelation and you will not find even one single case of any example, command, or necessary inference where musical instruments were used in the worship of the New Testament church.

I do not think this is an accident on God's part to design the worship of the New Covenant in this way. It is no more of an accident than having Christians meet on Sunday instead of Saturday like they did under the Old Covenant. God changed the music of the new religion, just like He did the day the congregation assembled.

The question now is, what kind of music do we dare to present to our God. Will we study the New Testament and search out the examples the Bible authorizes or will we design for ourselves worship that we are pleased with and let that be our Guide? If we choose to do this with the type music we present to God as worship, then there is no reason why we need to draw a line with any of the other ways we choose to worship God. And men have done, and are doing this very thing. Should we change the day of the week we assemble to worship God from Sunday to some other day? As you know, men have already done this. Consider the 7th. Day Adventists as an example. Should we change the Bible to some other book? There again, people are doing that, too.

The point is this; God designed the music we use to worship Him. Regardless of the reason why, He designed it to be presented to Him without the use of instruments, this is the pattern we are given in the Bible. If we present any other form of musical worship other than the way He designed it, we are guilty of presenting "counterfeit" worship. If we try to present worship to God that we have designed ourselves, it is rebellious sin, unauthorized by God.

The Bible tells us clearly the music we are to present to God as worship.

Colossians 3:16 (NKJV)
^{16} Let the word of Christ dwell in you richly in all wisdom, teaching and admonishing one another in psalms and hymns and spiritual songs, singing with grace in your hearts to the Lord.

Ephesians 5:19 (NKJV)
^{19} speaking to one another in psalms and hymns and spiritual songs, singing and making melody in your heart to the Lord,

Reading these verses gives a clear and precise understanding of the type music God has instructed us to present to Him as worship according to the pattern He has designed. We can clearly see that we are authorized to sing. And just so we can clearly see how this singing is to be presented to God, we can see that our singing is also described as "speaking". In another place it is described as "fruit of the lips". We also are told what type of songs to present. We are told to use psalms, hymns, and spiritual songs. Not only does this rule out musical instruments, it rules out "rock and roll songs", clapping, dancing and anything else you can name that is considered music that is not described in this pattern God has given us.

Would it surprise you to learn that instruments of music were not used in "church worship" for the first 600 years of church history? You can look this up for yourself if you would like. Look up **Pope Vitalian** on the internet under **Organ - Catholic Encyclopedia - Catholic Online**.

Pope Vitalian introduced the first instrument of music into the worship of the church. Up until that time all music of the church was singing in **a cappella form**. You may be familiar with the term **a cappella.** You know it means singing by using the voice only, without the accompaniment of any type of instrument. **But did you know that the word a cappella was an Italian word and it referred to "Chapel Music"?** It was so commonly known that the music of the church was non-instrumental that it was referred to as **a-cappella** style.

Stop and consider this for just a moment and think about what this means. It was very clear to the Christians of the original church that the music that God authorizes for the worship of the church is presented to God without the use of instruments. God specified **singing** and the original church understood what he wanted and followed the original pattern for the first 600 years of its existence.

Many people are surprised to learn this history and have never heard it before. I invite you to look this up for yourself.

Now that information may be strange to you and I hope it gives you cause to stop and think. But if that gives you reason to stop and think, the following information will really shock you. All the early reformers of Protestant denominations were against the use of instruments in public worship.

A quotation from the writings of John Calvin
"To sing the praises of God upon the harp and psaltery unquestionably formed a part of the training of the law and of the service of God under that dispensation of shadows and figures; but they are **not now to be used in public thanksgiving.**" (Calvin on Psalm 71:22)

The great reformer of the church, Martin Luther, wrote,
The organ in worship is the insignia of Baal... The Roman Catholics borrowed it from the Jews.
"Martin Luther," McClintock & *Strong's Encyclopedia*, **Volume VI, page 762;**

John Wesley, when asked about the use of the organ, replied, "I have no opposition to the organ in our chapel provided it is neither seen nor heard." **(Adam Clark's Commentary, Vol. IV, p. 868)**

Charles Spurgeon ... Baptist
(Spurgeon preached to 20,000 people every Sunday for 20 years in the Metropolitan Baptist Tabernacle and never were mechanical instruments of music used in his services. When asked why, he quoted 1st Corinthians 14:15. "I will pray with the spirit and I will pray with the understanding also; I will sing with the spirit, and I will sing with the understanding also." He then declared: "I would as soon pray to God with machinery as to sing to God with machinery." **(Charles H. Spurgeon, Baptist)**

Adam Clark, Instrumental Music, Law of Moses
Adam Clark: "I believe that the use of such instruments of music, in the Christian Church, is **without the sanction and against the will of God;** that they are **subversive** of the **spirit of true devotion**, and that they are sinful.

There are many others and their positions are readily available for anyone to see within their writings on the internet. If you choose, you can read the historical quotations for yourself.

As interesting as this information is, these are only the opinions of mere men. These men are highly respected in the world of religion for their contributions to the reformation movement, but only God has the authority to decide the type of musical worship He has asked us to present to Him. He has told us what type of music we are to use in our worship and He has revealed it to us in His Holy Word, the Bible. We are to sing. Look again at some of the verses that deliver this information to us and see if you are in agreement with what the Bible tells us to do. You will find no mention of using any types of musical instruments in any of the pages of the new contract we have with God. The new contract is the New Covenant or the New Testament as we refer to it today.

Let's look once more at some of these verses found there:

Ephesians 5:19 (NKJV)
[19] speaking to one another in psalms and hymns and spiritual songs, singing and making melody in your heart to the Lord,
Colossians 3:16 (NKJV)
[16] Let the word of Christ dwell in you richly in all wisdom, teaching and admonishing one another in psalms and hymns and spiritual songs, singing with grace in your hearts to the Lord.

Here are two passages where the inspired writers of God's Word have given us instruction for the type of music God has instructed us to use in our worship to Him. Look carefully at these instructions. You will see the subject matter of the type of songs we are to sing and you will find absolutely no authorization for musical instruments mentioned here at all. In fact, it is clear that we are to use our voices to present this music to God. Notice how it tells us to "speak these songs"? And notice, also, that we are authorized to "sing" and no other form of music or musical art is mentioned as being qualified to be presented to God as acceptable. **No wonder the original church and the early protestant reformers rejected the instrument as not being acceptable to use as worship to God.**

Carl O. Cooper.......On musical instruments in the church building

I would not go so far as to call "non-religious" instrumental music sinful. I do not think it is at all. But I do not think it is wise to introduce any form of an instrument into our buildings because of the impression and the message it sends to others including our children and grandchildren. I think it is like building a schoolhouse on the edge of a cliff. Everyone knows that no one would be hurt unless someone actually fell of the cliff. Now, everyone recognizes the danger of the cliff and no one would favor building a schoolhouse on the edge. We would be afraid that some child would accidentally fall over the edge of the cliff and be lost. We hesitate here and we protect. We see a real and genuine danger in the closeness of the cliff. Many people do not see a danger in instrumental music and the numbers are growing every year because their children live near the cliff.

The flirtation in the Church with instrumental music is like drinking "Near Beer". There is a beer that is brewed to taste and to smell like regular beer. It is not root beer. It looks like beer, it tastes like beer, it smells like beer, and it comes in bottles that look like beer. **But it is not alcoholic.** And no reasonable parent would set their children down to dinner and hand them a bottle of near beer and tell them to drink their fill. The reason they would not is not because they fear their child would get drunk, but because of the image it presents. The association the child would have to regular beer. There is a genuine fear of this associated image because parents know that regular beer represents a real and genuine threat to their child. Today, many in the Church do not see the introduction of instrumental music as a serious threat to the Church.

I have concluded that the doctrine surrounding instrumental music goes to the very heart of the core foundation of the Church of Christ. **The reason this doctrine can exist is because we are only free to do in worship to God what he has specifically authorized us to do.**

But we are not free to do those things which he has not specifically condemned. Almost all other religions teach that if it has not been specifically condemned then it is OK to practice. It is on this foundation footing, that we can only do those things specifically authorized, that the existence of the Church of Christ depends.

If we alter and disregard this principle then we would never be able to restore the original church because we would not be planting the "unaltered" true seed from which the original church of Christ springs forth.

Chapter 12
We are saved by grace

Our mental, physical, psychological, and genetic makeup, as well as, but to a lesser degree, our environment, determine our personalities. All this determines how we reason and how we react to the world around us. And this plays an important role in how we react to what the Bible has to say.

When we read about law and doctrine, faith and works, love and obedience, and grace, our personalities sometimes get in the way and cloud our understanding of the Bible's real message in all of these words. It is so easy for our personalities to determine where we will focus our emphasis, that we can miss the overall message. A tender hearted person, for instance, could place their emphasis on the acts of love and grace and completely miss what the Bible has to say about law, doctrine, and works. Another person might get so focused on doctrine that he completely forgets that the Bible also speaks of faith and love.

The truth is, in respect to our salvation and as to what is required by God for us to be saved, **every one of these words carries the weight of our salvation.** Our salvation depends on all of these things and we cannot be saved without them all. It is when we elevate one over the other that we create a problem. When one or two stands alone, more important and over the others, they will not save our souls.

We are saved by Grace. God has given us a plan of salvation whereby we can be saved. This was given to us by His grace. We did nothing to merit it, it was a free gift. God gave this gift to man from the goodness of His own heart, not because we deserved it at all. We are saved by the grace of God, but "grace alone" does not save. If that was so, then everyone would be saved. God has placed conditions on how this grace is distributed to man.

One of the conditions that God has placed on being able to receive forgiveness and justification by His grace is faith. We are told in Heb.11:6,

Hebrews 11:6 (KJV)
^{6} But without faith it is impossible to please him: for he that cometh to God must believe that he is, and that he is a rewarder of them that diligently seek him.

Faith is a very important prerequisite to having our sins forgiven. No matter what we do, without faith it is not acceptable to God.

But faith that leads us into obedience to God's instructions is the type of faith that saves. Obedience (works) saves us, but not without faith. (James 2:21-23) "Faith without works is dead" (James 2:20).

James 2:17-20 (NKJV)
^{17} Thus also faith by itself, if it does not have works, is dead.
^{18} But someone will say, "You have faith, and I have works." Show me your faith without your works,

> and I will show you my faith by my works.
> ¹⁹ You believe that there is one God. You do well. Even the demons believe--and tremble!
> ²⁰ But do you want to know, O foolish man, that faith without works is dead?

But what is the difference between law and works, are they the same? This is an area that confuses many people. If we cannot be saved by law, how then can we be saved by works? Works are obedience to law. Disobedience to law produces sin (1 John 3:4).

1 John 3:4 (NKJV)
> ⁴ *Whoever commits sin also commits lawlessness, and sin is lawlessness.*

If a man could perfectly obey law and therefore have perfect works, he would not need salvation, for he would have never sinned. God has always required that salvation be accomplished by works. Could Noah have been saved had he not obeyed God by building the ark? (1 Peter 3:20) Could Abraham have been saved if he had not offered Isaac as a sacrifice, as God commanded? (James 2:21). Can we be saved today without obeying God's gospel plan of salvation? God has always required works in order to be saved: but works without faith are useless.

Salvation without obedience is impossible. Heb. 5:9 tells us that Christ is the source of "eternal salvation to all who obey Him".

Hebrews 5:9 (NKJV)
⁹ And having been perfected, He became the author of eternal salvation to all who obey Him,

And "judgment is the outcome of those who do not obey the gospel of God". (1 Pet. 4:17) This "gospel of God" is doctrine. Can we be saved without the correct doctrine of God? No more than we can be saved without the correct gospel of God.

1 Peter 4:17 (NKJV)
¹⁷ For the time has come for judgment to begin at the house of God; and if it begins with us first, what will be the end of those who do not obey the gospel of God?

But what do we do about love? Isn't the Bible all about love? Surely if we have the love of God in our heart then God's grace will save us. Won't this over ride all this "rule keeping" philosophy? Why isn't love and faith enough?

There are so many different definitions of love. It seems there is a definition to suit any personality. The Bible definition of the love required for salvation is the same as obedience. 1 John 5:2-3 makes this exceptionally clear.

1 John 5:2-3
2. "This is how we know that we love the children of God; by loving God and carrying out his commandments.
3. This is the love for God; to obey his commandments".

We do not read about law and doctrine, faith and works, love and obedience, and grace all in one place in the Bible. They are highlighted in the areas where they are discussed. And sometimes we are told their great importance individually. But let us never think that standing alone, any one or two of these requirements is all we need. And let us not get "hung up" on any one to the neglect of the others. All are required by God to be saved.

Chapter 13
Living in a world hostile to Christians

How often has it been said that the church today is just not growing like it did in the 1950's? And it's true, we are not. And how often has it been said that our poor growth of 2014 is the fault of laziness on the part of Christians in the church today? It would seem that if we just knocked on a few more doors or if we could just invent the right program or if we just spoke the right words to our friends and neighbors that this growth of the past would be right back once again. But the truth is, we don't live in the same world today that existed in the 1950's. I lived then, and I saw the growth of the church in those days. I remember the discussions about the Bible in the barber shops and the drug store lunch counters. I remember how our brothers defended the restoration movement with book, chapter, and verse and how religious discussions were spontaneous and plentiful and how neighbors visited in each other's yards, and the schools and neighborhoods were quick to defend the moral principles found in the Bible. And there was genuine interest about the Bible by much of the population in general. It was a different time and the world was a different place.

And then the cultural revolution of the 1960's came. America was influenced and changed by racial tensions and by the fears of young America, of dying in a war. Few people would come out and say that they had a deep fear of war, and so the answer to that dilemma was to hold a political view that opposed the war. Politicians seized on this movement and used this emotion to create advantages for votes. Racial demonstrations and riots and political demonstrations and riots about the war took hold of young America and enhanced their rebellious youthful emotions and the result was a significant cultural revolution that has changed our America forever. We won't go back, ever again. In fact, deterioration of moral behavior and God fearing culture always feeds on itself and history shows us that before the pendulum starts to swing back, there is usually a major falling away.

And this brings us to our concerns today.

First off, let us resolve without any hesitation to never stop teaching the lost. No matter what happens, let us continue to teach the Gospel. Some will be saved, and the Bible commands us to teach and to evangelize the lost. Let us find new ways to teach the Gospel to those who are not saved, and let us use the internet and the air waves to teach and let us not grow weary in serving our God.

But our children will live in a world hostile to Christians. This seems inevitable by the evidence we can see. They are likely to face hostility from government sources and false religions as well. What would we advise them to do? First century Christians faced this and suffered. And as we can see from reading the Bible and from secular history as well, they suffered for their religious beliefs. And unless a miraculous event causes a major "turn around" in the culture of our time, a future generation will face this again.

There can be no "secret Christians". We are commanded to confess Christ as the Son of God and our Savior. To do less is to place our own salvation in jeopardy. And so the first thing we teach our children is courage, courage to serve our God no matter what. And commitment, complete and total commitment to the principles handed down to us from the apostles by the words of the Holy Spirit through the Bible. We need to teach courage and the commitment to hold on to our Faith and to do our duty as Christians no matter what. And regardless of what the future holds for any of us, these qualities will protect us from losing our souls.

We don't like to think about this kind of a future. We are fearful for our children and our grandchildren and so it's tempting to just accent the positive and to think on other things. Let us hope and pray that somehow, God intervenes and this deterioration of Christian tolerance by our nation and the world reverses itself and Christianity in our culture is preserved. But if nothing alters the rate at which we see this deterioration of Christian culture happening today, then may God help our future generations of Christians to exist in that environment.

If there is any hope in reversing it, or slowing it, it will be in teaching the lost to increase our numbers as best we can. Have you ever considered what it might be like if every church of Christ had a bill board on the highways? Suppose we all added the same message a thousand times everywhere you looked as you drove down the highways. And what about advertizing a message on TV? Saturate the air waves with the Gospel of Christ with TV ads and what do you suppose that would do? The point is this; there may be new ways to reach the lost.

If there is any hope in reversing it, or slowing it, it will be in teaching the lost to increase our numbers as best we can.

Another way to build up the number of Christians and to save more souls might be in establishing more schools of preaching. These schools are all over the world. I don't advocate supporting just any and every school. You need to support these schools after you have investigated their agenda and history. If you don't know how to do this, seek out a respected, conservative brother and ask for opinions and recommendations of which schools to support. I am not talking about Christian colleges. I am referring to schools of preaching. Training preachers to work on the front lines has an immediate result. Many of us will never teach or convert anyone else. This can be due to many factors. Some are legitimate and some are not, but using your own money to train preachers to go out into the field and preach the gospel is a way that guarantees some results. In fact, these young men might live many years after we are gone.

It is best if we all try to teach the lost. Do that as often as you can, but in addition to that, help with these other efforts in any way you can. But as you teach, remember this rule;

A. The proper way to teach is;
1. Give your student knowledge
2. This information will create emotion in the student
3. This emotion will lead to action based on knowledge

B. The wrong way to teach is;
1. Fill you student with emotion
2. This emotion leads to an action without knowledge
3. This action leads to error

The Bible tells us that we must worship God in spirit and truth.

John 4:23-24 (NKJV)
²³ But the hour is coming, and now is, when the true worshipers will worship the Father in spirit and truth; for the Father is seeking such to worship Him.
²⁴ God is Spirit, and those who worship Him must worship in spirit and truth."

We do not know what the future holds for any of us or for our descendents. But we need to teach our children and those we love that whatever we face, let us never be ashamed of the Gospel of Christ and let us have courage to stand and face whatever comes by declaring and confessing that Jesus Christ is the Son of God.

Chapter 14
Why People Seek Religion

People seek out religion for many and various reasons. Some come filled with fears, anxieties, and phobias and many are filled with high emotional stress. There are those who come filled with sadness and sorrows and are seeking relief from a life filled with grief. Some seek religion out of superstitious bewilderment and ignorance, and there are those who have been indoctrinated with irrational religious thoughts about what is supposed to happen to them by some religious experience or perhaps some mysterious action from the Holy Spirit.

All of these people are searching for something. Sometimes it is relief from some emotional distress, and others are searching for happiness or perhaps an elevated feeling of excitement which they perceive and conclude to be evidence of some "Spiritual" connection to a higher God.

When people come seeking religion with only these motives holding them to the church they are seldom satisfied with a worship service unless some level of an emotional need is met. We all have a need to find edification when we attend worship services, but there needs to be emotional edification properly balanced with worship that is done in "spirit and truth". When people come to the church to "get" rather than to "give" and when proper worship is engaged in by the congregation that fulfills God's pattern for worship that we find outlined in God's Word, the Bible; Seldom will their emotional needs be met. The type personalities described above will usually find satisfaction in a worship service designed around "therapy" styles of services designed specifically for the troubled personality who attends.

Services in denominational religious institutions and even in some churches of Christ have been changing over the years to create a "visitor friendly" type of atmosphere designed to suit the emotional needs of the people who attend. This is the theme and pattern of the typical Community church we find today on every corner and the plan does work to draw a crowd. Long ago it was discovered in sales training that if you want make a sale you have to give the people what they want and you have to wrap it up in a very pretty and appealing package that people like to look at.

It is very easy to allow a congregation to get caught up in this type of mindset as we seek to increase our numbers in our local congregations. It seems so right to equate our success as a church by counting the number of people who attend services on Sunday morning. And when we do that as a church, we become so afraid that someone might be offended by what we do that we stop doing anything that we fear might offend a visitor. This limits the sermons we present to only positive messages of love and gentleness and weakens and waters down God's teaching about the consequences of sin. In these cases we can become so wrapped up in presenting worship in "spirit" that we totally forget the worship that is supposed to be about "truth".

The people who come seeking religion with the types of needs I described at the beginning have a great need to be taught the truth. They need to hear sermons and Bible classes about God's pattern and design for the church and they need to know about the restoration of the "original church" and they need to understand the plan of salvation. They have a great need to know that God designed religion for mankind to properly worship Him, and all that we do in our worship is designed to bring honor and reverence to a Holy God. The worship we engage in is not to please ourselves, but is presented to please God.

We are not authorized to design worship to please the tastes and wishes of the people who set in the audience and to try to structure enough excitement to make sure they keep coming back. Many will not come back. Not because we want that to happen, but because we know from the parable of the sower found in Matthew 13 that all "ground" where the "seed" (The Word of God) falls will not be productive. In some ground the seed will just not grow. In those cases the people will not find what they are seeking and they will fall away. But we will try to save all we can. We must never redesign our services to "water down" the message for the purpose of keeping these people in our assemblies, but we should try everything we can to teach them what they need to know in gentleness and love.

It is a great thing when these people we have

described come into the church and are taught the Gospel and they are converted and baptized into Christ. This is what we are trying to do and this is the proper goal. But sometimes, due to a weakness in the leadership of the church, a person like this can pretend to be converted and disguise their true religious beliefs just to become a part of a group of people they have come to want to be around. This might not cause any problems in some cases and these people could sometimes attend the church for years and no one really know how they feel about the doctrine of the church. But it is very likely that the day will come when a more aggressive personality will rise up in the church and begin to introduce some error to the congregation. If this happens and it blends itself into the hidden views of the person who is not fully converted, a bond will likely develop between them. If there are others of like mind, the church is well on its way to a serious change.

This has already happened in many churches across our land. You can easily see the results in congregation after congregation that has allowed their teaching to drift farther and farther to the liberal left in religious doctrine. Most of the time this change is fueled by people who have a genuine desire to make their congregation a more friendly church, and more likely to get people to attend. But in every case it is done through ignorance and weak leadership of those leading the congregation. The start of this error is in a mindset that the worship service is for the purpose of evangelizing the lost.

Many times people have the mistaken idea that the

purpose of the worship service is to evangelize the lost. That is not the case. The purpose of the worship service is to reverently honor and worship our God. Sometimes the lost will attend. This is good when they do and we want to encourage this to happen, but we must never allow ourselves to become caught up in structuring our service around the lost people who happen to be in our midst. Those who bring visitors to the services should not expect things to change to please the ones who come and they should properly prepare them for what the service is all about.

I do not mean to imply that we should do things that intentionally insult those who visit. But in every case of conversion, there comes a point in time when the sinner has to understand and to realize things that they just did not understand. A person has to understand that he needs salvation and why he is lost in sin. They have to, at some point, understand that denominational division is sinful and wrong. They may have to hear that their respected relative's religion is not authorized in the Bible. They have to hear it proclaimed that there is a oneness to the church and the form and pattern of religion that God authorizes.

There will come a day when a visitor suddenly realizes and understands what is being taught. And when this light suddenly reveals the truth and it is understood, a decision has to be made. What will the visitor do? In some cases the Gospel takes root and a soul is saved and a life is won for God. But there are also other reactions as well. I know of some cases where the preacher is blamed for running away someone's friend or relative from the church because of what the sermon was about the day they came. I wonder about the conviction and intelligence of the member who reacts like this. Are they really converted to the doctrine of the church of Christ? What do they think should be taught? If enough of the congregation feels like this and would likely react like this, the members need more teaching and understanding of the basic doctrine of the church. This also reveals weak leadership in the congregation when there are people in the congregation who could react in that way. Nevertheless, many congregations fear this reaction so much they design and structure the service to see that this can't happen.

But let me caution everyone reading this, that it is possible for a preacher to give information in a sermon with many styles. Some preachers can deliver a message and tell everything they need to say in a gentle tone and never hold back any part of the things we believe, and offend no one. Yet there are other preachers whose delivery is crude and harsh and does offend. We should never hold back doctrine for the sake of visitors and yet we need to develop styles that say all we need to say and does not come across as crude, uncaring, and harsh. I know this can be properly done, because I have seen it happen. I attended a Gospel meeting some time back where the preacher invited his morning breakfast friends from McDonalds. He encountered them each morning when he went out to eat breakfast.

All of these people were from denominational churches of all kinds. My friend structured his sermon that day to deliver the message of the one church and the proper plan of salvation and he held no information back to please his denominational friends. We all understood that they were in the audience that day because he had introduced them as visitors and friends when he started. His sermon was done with gentleness and respect and not one person could have left that building who did not understand his message and not one person would have left offended because they thought they were attacked. I would add this as well, he did not apologize for the message of the Bible.

So it can be done. I heard another story about a young student preacher who decided to preach a sermon about a list of sins presented in the Bible. He expounded publicly on these sins using words to graphically describe what the sins were all about. The sermon was embarrassing and crude for the audience to hear. At the end of the sermon, two older preachers setting together in the audience started to get up to leave and one turned to the other and said, "well, what did you think about that"? The other old preacher said, "Well, even the Apostle Paul knew when to say, and such like".

And so what I am saying is this, we do not want to weaken our services to protect the ears of visitors with the exception that harsh, crude, and insulting sermons are out of place at any time.

Chapter 15
Reasons to Seek God

Well, with all this being said, what should our motives be for seeking God and religion? First off, there needs to be some intellectual reasoning involved. A person needs to come seeking God because he wants salvation and eternal life in Heaven. But this idea might be generated because of many reasons. Loneliness, failures, and grief will sometimes cause a person to search for a new direction in life that includes God. Many times people give no thought to Jesus and the church until they are brought low with the results of sin in their lives. The story of the prodigal son is a good example of this. You can find this story in Luke 15.

Now this may start out with a fear of Hell and eternal damnation. Sometimes a person may only know that something is lacking and missing with their relation with God and Jesus Christ. These are good and valid reasons for a person to come searching for answers and instruction in finding the religious path to Heaven. When this person comes into our midst we are blessed to have them there and we need to quickly do all we can to teach them what they need to know. It would be good if we had ongoing adult classes structured for this purpose, to teach beginners what they need to know to about the Gospel. If these classes are not available, someone needs to either go into their home or have them come to theirs, but they need to be taught. It is commonly known that if a new member or a visitor comes into our midst and does not make friends right away he will likely be lost to the world. Every member should make a genuine effort to make friends with new members and there should never be a visitor allowed to leave without the congregation speaking to him and befriending him anyway they can. This should be genuinely friendly and not just because someone is assigned to get this job done.

There are many cases when someone will come into our services with very little experience with Christian religion other than what little they have seen by observing behavior of family members and friends who claim a connection to some form of Christian religion. If this person has had no formal teaching about the Bible their world view is formed with whatever contact and experience they have observed. These experiences are almost always guaranteed and structured by the influence of Satan to help lead a person on a road to skepticism about religion in general. Most of the time these people are drawn to our services not because they are there to learn about the church of Christ, but because someone they care about has invited them to come. This is a great opportunity for this visitor to find a proper explanation about what it really means to obey the Gospel. If this person has a willing heart to hear and listen to what is being said in the Bible classes and if things are being said that piques his curiosity to know more, then he may be fertile ground for the Gospel to grow and produce fruit. This is why it is so important that our Bible classes and sermons from the pulpit actually deliver this information to those present. Not only do visitors need to hear these things but so do our own members as well. But even when this is done it still will not be enough. No matter if we are a visitor, a young person growing up in a church environment, or a faithful member of the church; if the only Bible study you get are the short intervals you have at church, it will not be enough. Every effort should be made to have Bible study in more ways than this.

If these personal Bible studies exist it will be an easy matter to invite anyone interested to participate in a personal way. This would be a great opportunity for a new member or a visitor to find friends and a "place" in his new environment.

There are many and various reasons why people who are seeking religion walk through the doors of the church of Christ. These reasons vary as much as the personality and mental ability of the people themselves. Some reasons are more credible than others but all bring them in contact with the Gospel of Christ. As in the parable of the sower in Matthew 13, they all have different ground where the seed of the Gospel is sown. The majority of these people will not allow this seed to take root and grow. We know that;

Matthew 7:13-14 (NKJV)
¹³ " wide is the gate and broad is the way that leads to destruction, and there are many who go in by it.
¹⁴ Because narrow is the gate and difficult is the way which leads to life, and there are few who find it.

If you have read this far you have more than a just a passing interest in what it means to be a member of the church of Christ. Perhaps you are already visiting a church of Christ somewhere. I have written these words with two groups in mind. I want to give information to those who want more knowledge about the church. I am hoping that there will be those who will give this book to someone they know who has questions about the church. And it is also for Members of the church who want to study these basic principles more.

Chapter 16
Will people be saved who are not members of the church of Christ?

This is a question that is asked a lot by people who are outside the church of Christ and who do not claim to be members of the church. As a general rule this question is asked not to actually try to get the answer but it is usually asked in a negative way to be critical of the church of Christ. But asking this question reveals several things about the person who is asking it. First off there is revealed a lack of understanding of who and what the church really is. And second there is revealed a lack of understanding of how one actually becomes a member of the church.

The Bible describes the church using many words and phrases. One way the church is described is by calling it "the body". Those who read and study the Bible understand that sometimes the church is referred to as the body.

Colossians 1:18 (NKJV)
[18] And He is the head of the body, the church, who is the beginning, the firstborn from the dead, that in all things He may have the preeminence.

The church answers to other names as well. Sometimes it is referred to as "The Kingdom of Heaven" or the "Kingdom of Christ". This is a good description of the church. The people who make up the church have Jesus as their King and as subjects they make up

Christ's Kingdom on this earth. So the church is the Kingdom of Christ.

The word church is an English word. The New Testament part of the Bible was not written in English but it was written in Greek. The actual Greek word used in Colossians 1:18 is;

Ekklēsia—Strong's Talking Greek & Hebrew Dictionary
The definition of this word is literally, "the out called". Or as we sometimes say, "those who are called out". And what is meant by that is, "those who are called out of the world from a life of sin to a life in the Kingdom of Christ, the church".

Those who are called out of the world into the church are those who are saved. Hardly any denomination would understand this. The reason they would not understand it is because their concept of the church does not allow it to be called the Kingdom of Christ. Many Protestant groups see the Kingdom of Christ to be a future prophecy yet to be fulfilled. This allows their definition of the church to be a "man made" organization that has been established as a temporary place of worship until the Kingdom actually comes. The Bible is clear in many places that this is not the case. Look at this scripture.

Colossians 1:13-14 (KJV)
13 Who hath delivered us from the power of darkness,
and hath translated us into the kingdom of his
dear Son:
14 In whom we have redemption through his blood, even
the forgiveness of sins:

Notice how this says we have been translated into the *"kingdom of his dear Son"*? So we are in the kingdom. But that's not all it says. Look at verse 14. Can you see that those who have been translated into the kingdom also have their sins forgiven? These people are the saved; those who's sins have been forgiven. Now that you also know these facts revealed in the Scriptures, would you say that the people who are in the church have been saved? You know, now, that they are.

But wait a minute. At what point do these people become a member of the church and which "church" do they become a member of? Could the many denominational churches be right when they say that once you are saved you must choose a church and join the church of your choice? But wait, we have already discovered that they all teach different and contradicting doctrines. Something is wrong here with this explanation. The Bible gives a different explanation for how we become members of the church, the kingdom of Christ. We are never told to join some church in the Bible. In fact, no one ever joins a church and no man has the authority to decide who is or is not a member of the church. God is in charge of who is added to the church.

Acts 2:40-41 (NKJV)
⁴⁰ And with many other words he testified and exhorted them, saying, "Be saved from this perverse generation."
⁴¹ Then those who gladly received his word were baptized; and that day about three thousand souls were added to them.

Acts 2:47 (NKJV)
⁴⁷ praising God and having favor with all the people. And the Lord added to the church daily those who were being saved.

So there it is. God adds people to the church. No man or no group has the authority to take away from God a process that He claims for Himself.

Which church does God add the saved people to? We have already discovered that the church is the ekklēsia, the called out. And we have discovered that the church is the body, and the kingdom of Christ. Look at this scripture;

Ephesians 4:4-6 (NKJV)
⁴ There is one body and one Spirit, just as you were called in one hope of your calling;
⁵ one Lord, one faith, one baptism;
⁶ one God and Father of all, who is above all, and through all, and in you all.

There is no more a multitude of bodies, or churches, than there would be multiple baptisms or Gods. The Bible declares for all to see; there is one body.

So now you know. When people are saved, God adds them to the church. How many people in the church are saved? You now know the answer. They are all saved. And to turn that around we could ask the question, are all the saved people members of the church? And the answer is still the same, all the saved are members of the church. Not "a church" but "the church". All the saved are members of the church that God adds them to. And we just read that there is only one. Does it surprise you to read these words in the Bible? Not many people understand this but it has always been a part of the Bible for people to read. But it contradicts the popular doctrine of "join the church of your choice". It does, however, uphold Jesus' last words in His prayer as He was about to die on the cross.

John 17:20-21 (NKJV)
²⁰ *"I do not pray for these alone, but also for those who*
will believe in Me through their word;
²¹ *that they all may be one, as You, Father, are in Me,*
and I in You; that they also may be one in Us,
that the world may believe that You sent Me.

Everywhere you turn when you study the Bible, you encounter the same teaching. There is a "oneness" with God, the church, baptism, and the doctrine we teach.

In the days following the death of Jesus on the cross there was one church. The apostles were united in their teaching and there was one Gospel. This was the original church and it was referred to as "the church of Christ".

Romans 16:16 (NKJV)
¹⁶ *Greet one another with a holy kiss. The churches of*
Christ greet you.

There was one original church with a congregation of members in every city. Gradually, over the years, there was a falling away from the original Gospel and the original church was perverted with many Gospels. But none of these new Gospels were ever approved by God. The Bible tells us this in no uncertain terms.

Galatians 1:8-9 (NKJV)
⁸ *But even if we, or an angel from heaven, preach any*
other gospel to you than what we have preached
to you, let him be accursed.

⁹ As we have said before, so now I say again, if anyone preaches any other gospel to you than what you have received, let him be accursed.

To change the original Gospel and to disobey Jesus' instructions through His prayer carries a serious penalty. The Bible says, *"let him be accursed"*. Men really don't pay attention to this prohibition and they create new Gospels anyway. Of course they are not really Gospels, people just think they are.

Galatians 1:6-7 (NKJV)
⁶ I marvel that you are turning away so soon from Him who called you in the grace of Christ, to a different gospel,
⁷ which is not another; but there are some who trouble you and want to pervert the gospel of Christ.

So what have we learned in these verses of Scripture we have studied? We learned that God established one original church into which all the saved are added by God as they are saved. This is the kingdom of Christ, the called out, the ekklēsia. This original church was one body and it taught one Gospel. The Bible sometimes referred to this church as the church of Christ. It is a great sin to change the one Gospel and try to change the doctrine to something new. Jesus, in His dying prayer, prayed for all men to be one and teach the same doctrine so that the world could believe that we are from Christ.

Chapter 17
The Great Falling Away

We have discovered already by reading the scriptures that God's design for the church is to be one body made up of the saved people of the earth. We are to be united in doctrine and purpose and we are to consider ourselves the kingdom of Christ.

In the beginning when the church was new and fresh there was no problem with the understanding of this concept. No one asked the question, "which church should I join", or "is one church as good as another"? There was one church and the saved were a part of it. It was referred to as "the church of Christ". There were congregations in every city where the Apostles and preachers evangelized the people and started one. This was the original church that God designed.

We can find the pattern for this church in the pages of the New Testament. This church can be restored today just as it was designed, if we follow the pattern for this design revealed to us in the Bible. If the rule book for playing baseball were lost for a thousand years and it was found again, could the game of baseball be restored? Of course it could be restored. By following the pattern for playing the original game, the same game the designer created can be played again just as the original game was played. And so can the original church be restored. All it takes is to rid ourselves of the books and creeds and prejudices of the religious world.

If we return to the Bible and use only the Bible as our guide to religious matters and if we only design the church according to the pattern we have revealed to us and we do not add things to what the Bible says just because we like it done our way. If we do that, the church can be restored to the original pattern and design that God gave us.

The church can be restored today just as it was in the days of long ago. This is the message of the church of Christ. This is a good message but is it likely that most men will follow it? It is not likely. It has always been the case that men will invent for themselves religions that please their own designs. Even from the beginning it was so. There have always been men who wanted to change the design.

The first cases of men who wanted to change the design came from the Jews in the days of the Apostles. These Jews were not motivated to try and honor and respect God by being obedient to His instructions about the design of the church. They were motivated with their hatred and prejudices against the Gentiles who obeyed the Gospel. For hundreds of years the Jews had nothing to do with the Gentile people and when they discovered that this new Christian religion extended salvation to the Gentile race, they wanted to redesign God's pattern for the church to force the Gentiles to become Jews. They tried to redesign the Gospel in order to force the Gentiles to become circumcised and obey parts of the old Jewish Law. This practice was severely criticized by the Apostles when the New Testament was written.

But there was a great falling away that led to a period of time we refer to today as the "Dark Ages" when the church God designed almost disappeared from off the face of the earth. This falling away was prophesied about in the New Testament. Look at some of what the Bible has to say about that.

2 Thessalonians 2:3 (NKJV)
³ Let no one deceive you by any means; for that Day will
not come unless the falling away comes first, and
the man of sin is revealed, the son of perdition,

Acts 20:29-30 (NKJV)
²⁹ For I know this, that after my departure savage wolves
will come in among you, not sparing the flock.
³⁰ Also from among yourselves men will rise up,
speaking perverse things, to draw away the disciples
after themselves.

This very thing did happen to the church. The false teachers who rose up and perverted the doctrine of the church were from within the church itself.

Within the first 300 years of the church men decided to redesign the organization of the church and allow men to rise up and take authority over more than one congregation. The original church had a group of elders to rule over each local congregation. This was the pattern we find in the Bible.

Titus 1:5 (NKJV)
⁵ For this reason I left you in Crete, that you should set
in order the things that are lacking, and appoint
elders in every city as I commanded you

The pattern for the ruling authority in the church is to have a plurality of elders in every congregation and the head of the church is Christ. These elders were never given the authority by the Scriptures to rule over more than one congregation. But men took on this authority by themselves early in the history of the church. This was the beginning of a great apostasy and the great falling away.

Not long after this false Gospel was invented, men decided to create a new structure for the complete organization of the authority in the church. The Pope was created as a mediator between the church and God. This was not supposed to be. The Bible tells us that there is one mediator and that is Jesus Christ.

1 Timothy 2:5 (NKJV)
5 For there is one God and one Mediator between God and men, the Man Christ Jesus,
This leaves no room for the office of a Pope in the church.

In this same process the church was reorganized to resemble the Roman Government. The office of Pope, Cardinal, Bishop, and Priests were all invented and added to the structure of the church. The Bible gives no authority for these new and invented positions of authority in the church.

All of this changing of the pattern for the church included a number of changes in the doctrine of the church as well. The new church that came to life during this time included all types of false practices and false doctrine. This was easy to enforce in these days because the clergy of the church wielded great power among the Governments of the land. And in addition to this, the Bible was not found in the hands of the common man. Only the clergy claimed the ability to read the Bible and it was not easy for a common man to check it out for himself.

This was the beginning of a long period of time in history when the original church almost disappeared.

But then the printing press was invented It was because of this invention that the Bible was able to be reproduced in ways that the average man was able to read it himself. As soon as this happened, men were able to see that the practices of this false church did not follow the teaching they could read about in the Bible. And many men set out to reform the church.

Now these few sentences cover many years of Bible history. I have no intention of making this book so detailed in this information that a person who is new to Bible study wears out on the details of this study. Anyone who wants a more detailed account can find this already in many books that exist for this purpose.

And so the first attempts to set the church right with what men read in the Bible were to try and reform the church to a closer agreement with the pattern found in the Scriptures. But many long years of false religious practices had already taken their toll on the world view and prejudices of men. And men had already formed religious doctrine around the doctrine already taught to them by the false form of religion that had been taught for many hundreds of years. It was very hard for these reformers to let go of these old doctrines they had held for years. There were some changes and many of the reformers saw different things that they thought the church needed to change. But none of them were united or in agreement with all the changes that needed to be made. And so it was that denominations were formed by reformers who disagreed on what should be reformed.

Over the years more and more reformers appeared on the scene and more and more denominations were formed. At some point they began to see division as something God approved of. They even went so far as to conclude that all of their doctrines were correct and God approved even when they contradicted each other.

The reformers started out with honorable motives but things got out of hand.

This brings us to the state of religious confusion the world is in today. There is a different brand of religion on every corner, all teaching a different and contradicting Gospel. None of this confusion and division in Christian religion is approved and authorized by God's word, the Bible.

The church of Christ has a plea, and that plea is to be united together into one church. That one church is the one church described in the Bible. It is the original church designed by God Himself. It is the church that God adds those to who are being saved. It is the Kingdom of Christ. It is the only church designed by God and there is no other. Let us restore that church as it was in the first century in the days of the Apostles and may we all be united as one.

Chapter 18
Can a saved person be lost?

This Question is asked many times because of a preconceived idea that has been implanted into people's minds from years of association with many denominational groups. This is the type of Bible information most people have accumulated as they go through life. Among the general population very few people would even question the religious information that seems official enough to come from preachers, pastors, and religious relatives. Little do they know that most of the religious information that is handed down does not come from actual Bible study, but from prewritten doctrine that is handed down through books and creeds and theology invented many years ago by the founders and reformers that started the denominations. One such reformer that is responsible for much of the religious doctrine found in denominational churches today is John Calvin.

John Calvin is the inventor of "Calvinism", which is taught as fact by most of the main stream denominations of today. Calvinism consists of 5 basic "laws" which deal with the salvation of man. These 5 "laws" are held up as "fact" by the leaders and pastors of most "protestant" groups. These 5 "laws" are, in fact, false and not true at all. Just a small amount of real Bible study will reveal that these 5 basic principal laws are not true. This doctrine is the foundation footing for the existence of many protestant groups. If, in fact, these basic foundation doctrines are false, the denomination no longer has a reason to exist

Here is an explanation of Calvinism from;

The New World Encyclopaedia
John Calvin *(1509 – 1564) was a prominent Christian theologian during the* **Protestant Reformation** *and is the namesake of the system of Christian theology called* **Calvinism***. In 1517, when Calvin was only eight years old,* **Martin Luther** *posted his 95 Theses.*
  John Calvin was a leader of the Swiss protestant reformation. Reformed and Presbyterian churches trace themselves from his reforms, while others including Congegationalist and **Baptist** *and the English Puritans draw on his theology.*
  Calvin is perhaps best known for the doctrine of predestination, Five points, making up the word TULIP, are used to summarize Calvin's doctrines:
  Total Depravity of Man*: That man's nature is basically evil, not basically good. Apart from the direct influence of God, man will never truly seek God or God's will, though he may seek the benefits of association with God.*
  Unconditional Election*: That God chooses or "elects" His children from before the foundation of time. God does not "look down the corridors of time to see what decision people will make"... rather, God causes them to make the decision to seek Him.*
  Limited Atonement*: That the death and resurrection of Christ is a substitutionary payment for the sins of only those who are God's elect children... not the entire world.*
  Irresistible Grace*: That when God calls a person, His call cannot ultimately be ignored.*
  Perseverance of the Saints*: That it is not possible for one to "lose his salvation."*
New World Encyclopedia

Out of the 5 basic doctrinal laws John Calvin invented and wrote into his description of the salvation and atonement of man, the one that seems to be the most notoriously known is;

Perseverance of the Saints: Calvin says it is not possible for one to "lose his salvation." This comes, in part, from this verse;

Romans 8:37-39 (NKJV)
37 Yet in all these things we are more than conquerors through Him who loved us.
38 For I am persuaded that neither death nor life, nor angels nor principalities nor powers, nor things present nor things to come,
39 nor height nor depth, nor any other created thing, shall be able to separate us from the love of God which is in Christ Jesus our Lord.

Sometimes this doctrine is referred to as **"Once saved always saved"**. You really don't have to turn very many pages in the Bible to find several verses that teach very plainly that this doctrine is not true.

Galatians 5:4 (NKJV)
4 You have become estranged from Christ, you who attempt to be justified by law; you have fallen from grace.

2 Peter 2:20-21 (NKJV)
20 For if, after they have escaped the pollutions of the world through the knowledge of the Lord and Savior Jesus Christ, they are again entangled in them and overcome, the latter end is worse for them than the beginning.
21 For it would have been better for them not to have

known the way of righteousness, than having known it, to turn from the holy commandment delivered to them.

In this section I have briefly covered only one of the 5 basic laws of "Calvinism". We could take the time to cover all 5 and we would see the same thing with them all, they are all just as false as this one is.

It is easy to study the Bible and read this for yourself. But it might not be so easy without a teacher to point it out more clearly. Find a teacher and study, but don't study without a Bible in your hand to prove what you hear.

I also think one of the most destructive points of Calvinism is the doctrine of; **Limited Atonement:**
*Calvin says; the death and resurrection of Christ is a substitutionary payment for the sins of **only those** who are God's elect children*

The reason I find this so disturbing is because it limits salvation to a certain group of people which God has already chosen through "predestination" before these people were even born.

This mindset, when taken at face value, prevents a person from even trying to read the Scriptures to find salvation for himself. Why should anyone search for the saving Gospel if their fate has already been determined by God long before they were born? If someone really believes this doctrine, there is no incentive to try to find salvation for themselves or for anyone else. What real difference would it really make?

And yet, this doctrine is so destructively false.

And not only is it destructively false, it is so easy to expose by reading the Bible. Look at these verses and make up your own mind. Does God prevent certain people from having a chance to be saved?

Hebrews 5:9 (NKJV)
⁹ And having been perfected, He became the author of eternal salvation to all who obey Him,

Mark 16:15-16 (NKJV)
¹⁵ And He said to them, "Go into all the world and preach the gospel to every creature.
¹⁶ He who believes and is baptized will be saved;

Here are 2 verses of Scripture that deny the truth of Calvin's doctrine of "predestination" and his doctrine of "limited atonement" as well. There are many more that we could quote but this is more than enough to show these doctrines are false.

Why do people believe these false doctrines and not check this out for themselves? The answer to that is complex. But the very basic problem comes down to just a lack of Bible study for themselves. Most people lack the motivation to start a real Bible study for themselves. It is so much easier to get their knowledge of the Bible is short sermons on Sunday and little "religious sound bites" that are picked up as we wander through life on our own.

It is not uncommon to find people who have attended church for many years and have really never read the Bible in a dedicated study for the purpose of learning if what they have been told is really true. Very few sermons in protestant, denominational churches center on the study of scriptures surrounding doctrinal text. Those doctrines such as the 5 points of Calvinism and the doctrines of their creeds and manuals will be taken at face value and neither questioned nor examined to discover if they are true. They are passed from generation to generation and never seriously investigated as you would think they should be. After all, there are the leaders of the "clergy" to handle that type of study and to make decisions for everyone else. And so, why worry?

But sometimes a person rises up who really wants to know more. For whatever reason, there are those who have a desire to know what the Bible wants them to do to be saved and to change their lives and live according to the pattern for our lives found and recorded in the Holy Book, the Bible. When a person has this desire, all members of the church of Christ are ready and willing to do all we can do to help.

That is why I have written this book. It is my intention to keep the concepts simple to understand. I do not intend to make the explanations long and complex so that a person new to Bible study will wear out on the explanations and discard the book before any Bible can be learned.

I hope that you can consider this book as a hand out to those friends and family members you feel would like to know more about the simple truth of the church of Christ and the New Testament Gospel.

You have been created in the image of God. There is within all of us a soul, and a subconscious knowledge and longing for a relationship with our Creator. And regardless of what you know and have been taught about religion, or even if you know nothing, there is still deep within your heart a yearning, a craving, to have a connection to Almighty God. Perhaps you know this or perhaps there is just that empty feeling as though something was not quite right and you are not just sure what it means. This book might be the starting point to help you see what you need to do.

But on the other hand, you may already have many years invested in a religion and you want to know more. You may have already discovered that many religions contradict each other in their doctrines, and you are questioning how these different doctrines can all be true. I don't blame you for wondering about that. That is the reason I have written this book. The plea of the church of Christ is "that we all unite as one body and teach the same thing". May we be "reconciled to God in **one body** through the cross"

Carl O. Cooper

2 Peter 2:20-21 (NKJV)
[20] For if, after they have escaped the pollutions of the world through the knowledge of the Lord and Savior Jesus Christ, they are again entangled in them and overcome, the latter end is worse for them than the beginning.
[21] For it would have been better for them not to have known the way of righteousness, than having known it, to turn from the holy commandment delivered to them.

Mark 16:15-16 (NKJV)
[15] And He said to them, "Go into all the world and preach the gospel to every creature.
[16] He who believes and is baptized will be saved;

Made in the USA
Columbia, SC
31 January 2025